WRESTLING JACOB

DECEPTION, IDENTITY, AND FREUDIAN SLIPS

IN GENESIS

WRESTLING JACOB

DECEPTION, IDENTITY, AND FREUDIAN SLIPS
IN GENESIS

SHMUEL KLITSNER

BEN YEHUDA PRESS
Teaneck, N.J.

Published by Ben Yehuda Press
430 Kensington Road
Teaneck, NJ 07666
http://www.BenYehudaPress.com

The cover image "Jacob's Angel" is reproduced courtesy of the collection of the Dennis and Phillip Ratner Museum, www.ratnermuseum.com.
Cover design by Larry Yudelson, based on a design by Shanie Cooper
Originally published in 2006 by Urim Publications.

CONTENTS

Introduction   11

1   Isaac's Abraham: Shall the *Blessings* of
the Fathers be Visited Upon the Sons?   40

2   Conditional Love and
the Purchase of Birthright   48

3   "I Am Esau":
Integrity and *Dis-integration* of Self   63

4   Of Dreams and Vows   78

5   In Laban's House   91

6   Preparations for Transition:
Geography as Psychological Territory   115

7   I Am Jacob   122

8   Human Autonomy versus Covenantal Destiny   143

9   Humility and Hubris:
The Donkey and the Bird   147

Afterword: Eden and Autonomy   177

ACKNOWLEDGEMENTS

I would be remiss if I did not thank the various friends who gave this book a close reading at various stages of its development and offered critique, advice, and the wisdom of their reactions. Particularly helpful were the responses of Henri Zukier, former professor of psychology at the New School for Social Research, Dr. Avivah Zornberg who has pioneered a sensitive literary application of psychoanalytic thinking to the biblical text, and Professor Meir Lockshin of the Judaic Studies department at York University who, as always, has been generous in giving his time and sharing his scholarship.

I would also like to thank several other readers of this work who offered editorial advice and encouragement, including Professors Daniel Schwartz, Yair Zakovitch, and Bob Brody of Hebrew University, as well as Charlie Buckholtz, Dinah Jehudah, and Noam Klitsner. Monday evenings at the home of Professor Moshe and Chava Greenberg have also been a source of inspiration and stimulating study.

Much of what I have been able to share with readers is a product of the years of training I was privileged to enjoy with the late Professor Nechama Leibowitz. Though much of what I've written was composed after her death, I did manage to discuss the reading of Exodus 4 with her in detail, and I was gratified by her positive response and blessing. Among the wise women from whom I have sought inspiration was also my grandmother Anna Traxler, who passed away on Passover 2003 at the biblical age of

110. The women who have contributed greatly to my understanding of these biblical passages also include the hundreds of challenging and highly motivated students at Midreshet Lindenbaum (Beruriah College) in Jerusalem where I have taught these past 22 years.

My wife, Judy Freistat Klitsner, thankfully shares my passion for bible study and is a gifted thinker and teacher. We have shared the challenges and joy of conquering many a biblical passage together as well as the ultimate joy and challenge of raising our five children. Much of this book is a joint product of our shared learning and discussion. God willing, we will continue to enjoy the years to come with Akiva and Ariella, Noam, Nechama and Eliad, Yisrael and Laurie, Amitai, and Mikey.

I gratefully dedicate this book to my father, Marvin Klitsner, of blessed memory. His kindness, wisdom, and moral and religious compass have forever changed our lives as we try to continue to navigate our journeys in his spirit. Together with my beloved mother—may God grant her long, healthy years—they raised children with love and devotion, and inspired in us a love of God and of Torah.

Shmuel Klitsner
Jerusalem 5767

A Note to the Reader

Numeration of verses is according to standard Jewish Bibles.

The Hebrew text is that of the Masoretic text.

Translations of biblical texts and commentaries are my own unless otherwise indicated.

Several traditional commentaries quoted throughout this work are quoted from the standard "Rabbinic Bible" *(Mikraot Gedolot)*. For some quotations of commentaries not always found in Mikraot Gedolot, specific editions are cited.

A working knowledge of biblical Hebrew will certainly enhance the reading of these chapters, though I have endeavored to make it readable as well for the audience that is restricted to a reliance on English translations. Undoubtedly, the best way to read this book would be with a Hebrew Bible at one's side.

The introduction to this work is intended for readers who generally appreciate, or require understanding of, the author's methodological premises before reading the work itself. Others should feel free to begin their reading with Chapter One.

INTRODUCTION

Let me state at the outset that this work is that of a student of the biblical text. I have no formal training in psychology or philosophy beyond the appetite for the classical wisdom of those fields that typifies many enlightened modern readers of the Bible. As such, rest assured that I arrive at the text with no specific psycho-literary methodology. I will not impose upon the text a Freudian or any particular post-Freudian theory of interpretation. In fact, there are only two litmus tests in this work for the validity of an insight. Does the idea seem to emerge from a close reading of the text? Does the idea resonate with a common sense, intuitive understanding of human nature (albeit an understanding informed and enriched at times by the insights of modern psychological sensibilities)?

For example, one should note that my use of the term repression is not always the Freudian one that speaks of impulses suppressed by the super ego; but almost the inverse, at times. The Genesis narratives seem to imply at various junctures that Jacob's impulses—and his attempts to advance a perceived divine plan—often suppress his inner moral voice. Thus, by *repression* I mean the relegation of something from the conscious to the unconscious, a colloquial sense of something sent from the living room of the mind into the cellar. I use this term without a claim as to what does the relegating and what it is that is sent to the "basement" of the soul.

There is also no attempt to impose the oedipal conflict upon the narratives. In fact, at one point it seems to be reversed as the mother Rebecca becomes the authority figure who inadvertently complicates Jacob's path to the much desired relationship of love with his father, Isaac.

In short, while aware of the recent proliferation of psycho-literary theories and methodologies, I have chosen to take my lead—as exclusively as possible—from the idiosyncrasies of the text. The limited deployment of formal psychological categories is intended analogically, as a way of elucidating for the modern reader those insights that seem to both emerge from the text and to resonate with common experience and intuition.

Close Reading and Characterization

One might expect a book of close readings of biblical texts to resemble the Freudian readings of Greek myths. In that well known genre as well, writers peruse the epic tales to cull their anthropological conceptions and to inform our own understanding of ourselves. But as Robert Alter has noted, biblical writing departs radically from "the fixed choreography of timeless events" and moves toward the indeterminacy of ambiguities that "resemble the uncertainties" of life and of history.[1] For Alter and other close readers of the Hebrew Bible, it is this shift that allows a transformation of the narrative art from "ritual rehearsal to the delineation of the wayward paths of human freedom, the quirks and contradictions of men and women seen as moral agents and as complex centers of motive and feeling."[2]

Thus, biblical heroes are very different from the epic heroes in that they live and breathe and struggle and fail and transcend in real situations. They instruct not in their mythic stature but in their human complexity, not in their succumbing to or tragically resisting a fated destiny, but in a tortuous negotiation between their flawed interiority and their divine covenantal calling.

---

[1] R. Alter, *The Art of Biblical Narrative* (NY: Basic Books, 1981) 25–27.
[2] Ibid.

In fact, we will suggest that the book of Genesis stands in opposition to the Greek epics in the following way as well: In the Greek epic, the hero falters in his futile attempt to ignore the fate set for him by the gods. By contrast, in some of the Genesis narratives, the heroes and heroines falter in their inappropriate sacrifice of moral autonomous judgment to the dictates of a perceived divine plan. The Greek hero is unaware of his inescapable fate; his autonomy is an illusion. The biblical heroes are aware of their covenantal destiny, but cannot escape their autonomy. This double bind of *moral responsibility vs. covenantal destiny* is particularly evident when biblical characters try to advance the divine objective in ways that bypass their own integrity.

Literary approaches to the Bible have noted the crafted artistry of the narrative mode that so resembles the modern development of narrative art. Yet, it is also abundantly clear that the Hebrew Bible communicates its stories using tools that are rarely used by moderns—and with an economy of description that is deceptive in its subtlety and begrudging by standards of the modern reader.

Though Alter has led the most recent battle against anachronistic expectations of the biblical text, he is also among the most forthright of scholars in declaring that:

> "Biblical narrative offers us, after all, nothing in the way of minute analysis of motive or detailed rendering of mental processes; whatever indications we may be vouchsafed of feeling, attitude, or intention are rather minimal; and we are given the barest hints about the physical appearance, the tics and gestures, the dress and implements of the characters, the material milieu in which they enact their destinies. In short, all of the indicators of nuanced individuality to which the Western literary tradition has accustomed us. . . would appear to be absent from the Bible."[3]

---

[3] Ibid, 114.

Yet, merely because the modern literary means of denoting character are largely absent, one is not best served by assuming the absence of characterization. The narratives of the Hebrew Bible constitute a unique literary genre with their own balanced blend of plot, character, and message. It has long been noted that the range of meanings of these texts must be explored with sensitivity to the subtle uses of language and style that are peculiar to this genre. Thus, scholars have debated the relative priority of plot, character and message in these narratives as well as their relationship to historiography. Perhaps because of a bias of modernist expectation, many recent exegetes, even those with a literary approach to the biblical text, have downplayed the role of presentation and development of character.

Even some of the most keen literary readers of the Bible, like Yair Zakovitch, have suggested that the reason for the sparse information and seeming neglect of characterization is the subordination of character to other interests of the writer:

> "For the biblical narrator the portrayal of personality is never the main theme; for the most part, the human being is a vehicle to transport the history of a nation in its relationship to its God...."[4]

What seems to run counter to this general statement is the extent to which biblical heroes frequently and decidedly do *not* serve the thrust of the divinely mandated destiny. On the contrary, they often seem to inhibit the divine plan, and more often than not, these characters struggle to navigate between their own very human limitations and the prophetic

---

[4] Y. Zakovitch, *David: From Shepherd to Messiah* (Jerusalem: Yad Ben Tzvi, 1995) 10 (my translation from Hebrew). This remark is particularly surprising as it appears in the introduction to a book that is framed as a biography of a biblical character, which is in itself a rare, nearly anomalous form of commentary.

vision they are meant to advance.

In fact, it would seem that the real drama of the biblical text lay precisely in the thorny complexity of intensely human (and at times tragically faulted) heroes functioning in the arena of morally ambiguous interaction with friends, family and foes and simultaneously in the orbit of a divine covenant.

Less categorical than the above statement, yet still open to critique, is the observation of another skilled contemporary literary exegete, Uriel Simon. He distinguishes between primary and secondary characters in biblical narratives by suggesting that secondary characters should be defined as those that simply serve the interests of the plot or as foils to highlight or contrast the important traits of the primary characters.[5] This claim—while undoubtedly accurate in many cases—becomes problematic when deployed as a sweeping rule that supposedly obviates the need to engage so-called secondary characters with the tools of close reading. An unfortunate example of this is Simon's treatment of Isaac's return from his near sacrifice atop Mt. Moriah. Simon claims that what seems to many readers—from ancient times to the present—a striking gap in the narrative of the *Binding of Isaac* (Gen. 22), is no more than "a classic stylistic instance of the subordination of the secondary character Isaac for the needs of the story."[6]

In this way, Simon does away with the need to relate literary significance to the absence of Isaac on the return from Mount Moriah; this, despite the repeated phrase, "and the two of them walked together" (referring to Abraham and Isaac) in the verses describing their ascent to Moriah. The fact that in the descent Isaac is absent, yet the lads who wait throughout the drama at the foot of the mountain "walk together" with Abraham on the way back, is also not deemed a sufficient literary indicator to deserve attention in a *"plain sense"* reading. It seems that beyond *subordinating* Isaac to the "needs of the story" as a mere secondary character in the story

---

[5] See Uriel Simon, *Kriah Sifrutit BaMikra* (Jerusalem: Mosad Bialik, 1997) 320.
[6] Ibid (my translation of the Hebrew).

of the *Binding of Isaac,* Simon has actually *sacrificed* a close reading of the character Isaac upon the altar of predefined exegetical categories.[7]

In the course of my own analysis of the character of Isaac, I will attempt to show the profound significance of the absence of Isaac from the descent from Moriah and the resonance of this gap in subsequent Isaac stories.

The late Jewish philosopher and poet, Abraham Joshua Heschel, coined a phrase that accurately stands in opposition to the assumption that biblical characters, primary or (so-called) secondary, merely service the plot or history for the biblical authors. Heschel claims that the Bible should be read as "*divine anthropology.*"[8]

Every reading of the Bible presumes a prior conception of the nature of the books being subject to examination. For Heschel, and I believe for Robert Alter (though from different perspectives), the narratives of the Bible are primarily about what it means to be human in a world confronted by the divine call. As such, there is no more significant feature of the text than the way its heroes and villains negotiate their destinies. Their foibles as well as their successes are the stuff through which the text communicates its story. If we fail to perceive the subtle indicators of individuation and the exquisite twists and turns of character development that often lie "hidden in plain sight," we do not simply fail to add a speculative layer of *overinterpretation* to the history, or prophetic message, or plot.[9] We risk ignoring the center stage and focus of this subtle work of divine anthropology.

What *are* the subtle indicators and idiosyncratically biblical methods for conveying motivation, attitude, feeling, and moral quandary? For as

---

[7] In fairness to Simon, he is, in this particular case, following in the footsteps of the 12th century exegete Ibn Ezra in the latter's comment on Genesis 22:19: "And Isaac was not mentioned because he is subordinate to him [Abraham]."

[8] Abraham J. Heschel, *Man is not Alone* (NY: Farrar, Straus and Giroux, 1976) 129.

[9] For debate concerning this term, see Umberto Eco, *Interpretation and Overinterpretation* (Cambridge University Press, 1992).

Alter has astutely noted: The markers of individuality preeminent in the novel, "but ultimately going back to the Greek epics and romances," are indeed mostly absent from the biblical narrative.

Before describing some of the literary tools I have employed in trying to understand the biblical narrative technique in the Jacob stories, I want to venture a comment on the odd convergence of two opposing agendas. It may strike one as perverse to suggest that Jewish fundamentalist readings of the Bible and secular historical readings share the same disadvantage. Yet, experience with both biases leads one to this observation. For many in the historical school, the literary character of biblical heroes is subordinated to a presumption of the text as a primitive composite of ancient traditions woven into an ideologically motivated text—fraught with scribal omissions, errors, and awkward repetitions. Needless to say, this presumption all but precludes the possibility of viewing unusual word choice, ellipsis, creative ambiguity and repetition as subtle and purposeful indicators of meaning. Inevitably, for this school of research, biblical characters will also not be seen as subjects for the kind of close reading that pays attention to slips of tongue (or quill) in their dialogue. Unusual or anomalous language that is used to describe their actions will also not merit the kind of interpretation that Freud applied to both speech and behavior.

Oddly enough, the modern fundamentalist Jewish religious reading also frequently refuses, on its own ideological grounds, to see the text as a stylistically crafted work. For these fundamentalist readings, a divinely written text will present heroes and heroines who transcend the possibility of human folly. Once characters are more than human, they are also not individuated, as their divinely imbued missions eclipse all idiosyncrasy and make irrelevant, or inadmissible, any indications of struggle and failure. In such a scheme, biography becomes hagiography and the subtleties of character are once again subordinated, this time to the grand strokes of an unambiguous divine message. For the fundamentalist reader, to speak of the tragic flaws of Abraham or Isaac or Jacob is tantamount to the tarnishing of the "image of the Almighty."

Moreover, when it comes to the analysis of perceived ambiguities or repetitions in the text, all of these must be resolved as illusory; they will *not* be seen as purposeful literary indicators bearing artistic value and meaning. The result: neither the assertion of an essentially primitive historical text nor that of a divinely "infallible" text allow for the middle ground of subtlety that draws its sustenance from the very same oddities and anomalies that one school denies and the other takes as scribal error or shoddy redaction.

On Anomalous Language or Slips of Quill

Classic biblical commentaries have always focused on puzzling grammatical and syntactical constructions as well as deciphering and analyzing odd or anomalous word choice. Most often, the thrust of the comment on any difficult word or phrase is to "solve" the problem by explaining why, upon deeper reflection and in comparison to other biblical uses of the term, the words are indeed the *right* ones to have been written. Bible critics, focusing on the same phenomena, often suggest that the words may in fact be the *wrong* ones and then proceed to suggest textual emendations that are often speculative as to what the original uncorrupted text might have been.[10]

---

[10] Clearly, much of the literature regarding textual emendation is well grounded in ancient manuscripts such as the Samaritan Torah and the Dead Sea Scrolls. Yet, the analysis of the masoretic text as is, need not be entirely replaced by a preferred reading of a variant text. See the commentary to the Torah of N.H. Tur-Sinai, *Peshuto Shel Mikra*, for an extreme example of a modern Jewish commentary that consists almost entirely of resolution of textual difficulties through emendation. Notwithstanding the principle adopted by many scholars of *lectio difficilior*—that argues that the more difficult reading is paradoxically, most often the authentic reading—the urge to emend in order to *read more plainly* persists unabated and remains typical of many exegetes. (See also the fascinating work of Timpanaro, *The Freudian Slip: Psychoanalysis and Textual Analysis,* 1974—which argues against

I would propose a third approach that if applied judiciously may bear surprisingly fruitful exegesis. Let us assume that the text should be read as is. I mean this in two ways. On one level, let us not *solve* the difficult language by emending it. But let us also not rush in to *resolve* the difficulty by suggesting how we might understand the words to be the *right* ones. Instead, let us don the mantle of Freudian interpretation of language and resist solving or correcting the language. We will, rather, *embrace* the difficulty as reflecting a subtext of meaning and as an opportunity for deeper revelation of the full literary payload.

To put it directly, I am suggesting that the relationship of text to subtext is best explored when there *are* rough readings, non-sequiturs, anomalous word choices, ungrammaticalities and jumbled syntax. By smoothing over the bumps and removing the obstacles, we provide an easier ride but risk overlooking a rich landscape of subtext that lurks beneath the surface and is often hidden between the lines.

Many will readily identify this method of close reading with that of the classic, Rabbinic midrash as explained by Daniel Boyarin, wherein the semiotic claim (not just the theological one) is that "if God is the implied author of the Bible, then the gaps, repetitions, contradictions, and heterogeneity of the biblical text must be read...."[11]

I want to claim, however, that in a literary close reading that follows the lead of Freudian interpretation of language, the subtexts are implicit within the language of the text itself. These subtexts, can be excavated without resort to the importing of external gap filling and artificial resolution that often typify the midrashic reading. Indeed, if the distinction between the *plain sense* reading *(pshat)* and the midrashic one is that between reading into a text and reading out of a text, one would be justified in deeming

---

lectio difficilior and suggests a more prevalent form of accidental scribal error that he calls banalization.)

[11] Daniel Boyarin, *Intertextuality and the Reading of Midrash* (Indiana Univ. Press, 1990) 40.

these close readings "literary *pshat*," to borrow a phrase from Uriel Simon.[12] Ultimately, whether the claim of implicit subtext to any given verse will be judged as a literary reading, as creative midrash, or (in the least charitable view) as *overinterpretation,* will depend on the resonance of the subtext with the literary whole and upon the further contextual indications of such subtext.

While the distance between a psychological close reading and the midrashic method is largely a matter of the degree of contextual support, it should be clear that the method of classic medieval Jewish commentaries stands in opposition to the Freudian agenda of embracing difficult language.

In a conversation with the late Nehama Leibowitz,[13] I asked for her understanding as to why the classic commentaries of Rashi, Nachmanides, and others generally satisfy their agenda with the resolution of textual difficulties. Except in the case of apparent redundancies, they rarely proceed to address the question of why the difficulty was in the text to begin with. Her response was that Rashi and his successors viewed these difficulties as arising only by virtue of the reader's inadequacy, and not as a result of a purposeful ambiguity or anomaly in the text itself. She added for good measure that even in her own writings, wherein she made it second nature for modern students to ask "what is difficult in the verse for Rashi?" what was meant was **not** the need to find an inherent difficulty but rather to locate the **appearance** of difficulty addressed by the commentary. We proceeded to discuss various verses in which Leibowitz had herself pointed to the artistic use of ambiguous pronouns in the biblical text. As a result,

---

[12] Readers will judge whether I have borrowed the phrase "literary *pshat*" or hijacked it. (Certainly, in his own commentary, Simon employs his own sense of literary *pshat* in a much more restricted and cautious manner.)

[13] My revered mentor, Prof. Nehama Leibowitz, is best known for her five volumes of *Studies of the Five Books of Moses,* published by the Torah Education Dept. of the World Zionist Organization. Her expertise was the analysis of the methodologies of the classic medieval commentaries, particularly Rashi.

she softened her stance, but maintained nonetheless that the reason for the silence of the various medieval exegetes (concerning the underlying motivation for textual difficulty) was their presumption of a plain speaking, infallible, divine text. This conception, for the most part, ruled out the possibility of looking for purposeful anomaly and ambiguity.

In contrast, the method of exegesis employed in this work regards textual difficulty as inherent in the text and as a primary indicator of latent meaning.

Certainly, there is by now a small library of literary criticism that discusses the correlation of exegetical examination of subtext and the Freudian analysis of the subconscious. Susan Handelman, in her seminal work on "the emergence of rabbinic interpretation in modern literary theory," has traced the connection between the Rabbinic understanding of latent and manifest content of holy texts, and Freud's understanding of the latent and manifest content of dreams.[14] In fact, Freud himself remarked that in his interpretation of dreams—as in that of parapraxis (the Freudian slip): "we have treated as Holy Writ what previous writers have regarded as an arbitrary improvisation, hurriedly patched together in the embarrassment of the moment."[15] As Handelman notes, "For Freud, what looked illogical was only so (as in the case of the written Torah) because the text is truncated, lacunary, but nothing in it is arbitrary, senseless, or out of place...."[16]

Avivah Zornberg was correct, as well, in pointing out that "the midrashic search for multiple levels of meaning" is in effect "an attempt to retrieve unconscious layers of truth." She is also justified in stating that "the psychoanalytic project, like the midrashic one, represents a dissatisfaction with surface meanings, and a confidence that rich if disturbing

---

[14] Susan Handelman, *The Slayers of Moses* (Albany: SUNY Press, 1982).

[15] Sigmund Freud, *The Interpretation of Dreams* (New York: Avon, reprinted 1965) 552.

[16] Handelman, 148.

lodes seam the earth's depths."[17]

Yet my contention is that the surface ripples that run through the Bible—when its passages are subjected to tight contextual analysis—do more than merely point to the possibility of midrash. The textual quirks that midrashic writings often exploit for the purpose of an impressionistic expansion of the text can also provide the stuff of close reading and philological micro-surgery. While the midrashic approach is also ultimately based on the indication of subtexts within the text itself, I hope to demonstrate throughout the book a different interpretive stance that consistently sees textual anomaly as indicative of subtext, and subtext as often indicative of internal motivation. Moreover, that motivation is sometimes portrayed as unknown or unconscious on the part of the main characters. This is what is meant by my claim of subtext as subconscious.

Subtext and Subconscious

There is need to further clarify the suggestion of subtext as subconscious, lest it be misunderstood as shifting the focus of relationship between text and commentary. We do **not** mean to say that the exegete should stand above the text and presume to understand latent strata of the written medium that remain hidden from the authorial voice. We are not speaking of the classic Freudian mode of interpretation wherein layers of meaning become known even to the author only through the analysis of an outside ear that listens to that voice and pays special attention to the peculiarities that riddle it (and sometimes make it into riddle.) While this may constitute an appropriate and worthwhile approach for much of literature, we do not propose that this characterize our reading of the Bible.

Even putting aside the issue of divine or prophetic authorship, I part ways with certain psychoanalytic readings of the biblical text when they begin to presume an understanding of authorial intent, or authorial subconscious bias. For me, as well as for the traditional classic commentaries

---

[17] Avivah Zornberg, *The Particulars of Rapture* (NY: Doubleday, 2001) 6–7.

of Rashi, Nachmanides on the one hand and for secular literary readings like those of Robert Alter on the other, the text becomes either sacred or sacrosanct in that we accept it as it is. The text speaks, not the author, and the way the text speaks is through the mutual communicative process of conversation between the written word and the investigative reader. This is the stance of the Talmudic generations that use phrases like *"hakatuv omer," scripture speaks,* and this is the stance of the most sensitive secular literary readers of the Bible, who humbly accept the integrity of the text while freely and fully interpreting its literary complexity.

In this regard, one should consider the remarkable allegorical passage in the Babylonian Talmud (Tractate *Menachot* 29b), in which Moses has ascended Mt. Sinai only to discover that God is not quite ready to deliver the Torah. He is busy attaching crowns to the tops of the letters of the Torah that will only be interpreted generations hence by Rabbi Akiba. These crowns remain incomprehensible to Moses himself. In the introduction to his legal responsa, the late Rabbi Moses Feinstein, preeminent decisor of Jewish law in the latter half of the last century, offers a surprisingly postmodern (yet quintessentially Rabbinic) explanation of the passage. For Feinstein, the crowns on the letters represent sovereignty, and God himself in this midrashic allegory—by crowning the letters—grants sovereignty to the text to speak in ways that will be understood differently in each generation, and in different ways than those intended by God himself as author. Thus, even in traditional rabbinic discourse, authorial voice and intent become muted and irrelevant before the sovereignty of the text and the dynamics of its dialogue with the readers of subsequent generations.

(Even with regard to an author with a well known biography, one would be on shaky and less fertile ground in looking at his life and times and his idiosyncratic biases to illuminate his writing, rather than looking at his writing in order to understand the writing. How much more apt is this limitation when applied to the biblical text whose authorship will always remain shrouded in either the ambiguities of ancient history or the mysterium tremendum of the prophetic medium.)

Having said this, what *is* meant by *subtext* reflecting *subconscious* is the analysis of the text's rough edges as subtexts that reflect the motivations of biblical characters and the ironies of the narrative.

We will find ample evidence of the subtle use of unexpected or *"wrong"* language to indicate what may be the hidden motivations of our biblical heroes and villains, just as the use of odd language that is borrowed from other biblical texts is often used to communicate the latent layer of meaning through an artistically intentional use of intertextual reference.[18] Let me illustrate both these psycho-literary phenomena with an example not taken from passages dwelt upon in the book.

In the second chapter of the book of Job, after the hero has suffered the loss of his children and the destruction of his house, he is smitten with boils from head to toe and sits amidst the ashes, scratching his flesh with a shard of clay. All of this, of course, has befallen him as part of God's wager with Satan that the well-blessed Job would continue to be a righteous man and at the very least would *not* curse God, even in the face of disaster. At this point, the friends of Job enter the story as they have gathered to come to Job to console him:

---

[18] George Savran has distinguished between two different usages of the term "intertextuality" in literary analysis: "In the broadest sense, the expression 'intertextuality' implies a general recognition that 'every text is constrained by the literary system of which it is a part, and that every text is ultimately dialogical in that it cannot but record the traces of its contentions and doubling of its earlier discourses'" (D. Boyarin, *Intertextuality and the Reading of Midrash*, Indiana U. Press, 1990, p. 14). But the term also has a more limited significance... namely, an examination of the interaction between the specific text which is the object of study, and one or more additional texts—the intertext. G. Savran in *Journal for the Study of the Old Testament 64* (1994) 36. Also see Savran's note 12 there, which refers to theoretical literature on intertextuality. It is the narrower use of the term that is employed in Savran's article there ("Intertextuality, Baalam's Ass and the Garden of Eden"), and it is this same use of the term that I employ in the following chapters.

"And they lifted their eyes from afar and did not recognize him.
And they raised their voices and they cried. And they tore each
one his cloak, and they *threw dust upon their heads heavenward.*
They sat with him on the ground for seven days and seven nights
and did not speak a word to him for they saw that his pain was
great."

The description of the behavior of Job's friends is anomalous and requires explanation. In nearly all other biblical descriptions of grief or
consolation, the expressions of empathy or mourning are fewer.[19] Only
here do we find raised voices in crying, rending of garments, dust upon
the head, sitting on the ground and prolonged silence all in one passage.
Furthermore, in all other cases of dust upon the head as expression of
mourning, the dust is *placed* upon the head—never *thrown* and certainly
not thrown *heavenward!* The exaggerated description may be taken as
simply reflecting the exaggerated circumstances of Job's misfortune or
alternatively as reflecting an ironic use of hyperbole. Support for the latter
interpretation comes from an unexpected coincidence of phrasing between
this passage and the words used to describe one of the ten plagues in the
ninth chapter of Exodus, verses 8–10:

"Then the Lord said to Moses and Aaron: Take you handfuls of
soot of the kiln and have Moses *throw it heavenward.* . . and it shall
become upon the humans and the beasts as boils. . . and Moses
threw it heavenward and it became boils. . . ."

The intertextual reference in Job to the prior, well-known passage in Exodus creates literary superimposition of one text upon the other; its anoma-

---

[19] The sole exception seems to be the passage in Ezekiel 27:30–32, though the context
there is not a narrative of actual suffering and grief, but rather a dire prophecy of
woe that is to befall a foreign city.

lous phrasing creates a subtext of meaning that must be analyzed.[20]

Why would the author of Job send us running to Exodus, associating an act of throwing dust heavenward as consolation for boils (and other emotional grief) with an act of throwing ashes heavenward that actually produces a plague of boils? It would seem that the explanation lies in a broader contextual look at the relationship between Job and his friends as expressed in the next forty chapters of the book. Though apparently well intentioned, the friends are constantly causing further grief to the suffering Job by telling him that the painful existential problem confronted, namely the theodicy of the suffering of the righteous, need not cause him additional pain. For them, the suffering can be explained either by redefining the status of Job as less than righteous or by redefining his suffering as kindness that cannot be discerned from a limited human perspective. It is apparently because of these insensitive and misguided assertions that the friends of Job are admonished by God at the end of the book.[21]

There could be no better way of foreshadowing the well intentioned but egregiously insensitive way in which the friends' very attempts at comforting Job, in fact, bring him further pain, than by telling of an initial act of consolation that also bears the irony of conflict between intent and effect. Through the similarity of language that points to a superimposition of one text upon the other, the friends' act of consolation for Job's boils refers us back to another passage in which the same act actually inflicts the very same affliction of boils.

One might suggest as well that the exaggerated number of expressions

---

[20] Meir Weiss, in his wonderful essay, *The Beginning of the Book of Job* (Jerusalem: Magnes Press, 1983) 76, notes the intertextuality here, but disappointingly attributes the phenomenon to an ancient superstition that if a certain symbolic action can precipitate a negative result—a parallel or identical action may be capable of reversing the effect. For Weiss, then, the friends may be acting symbolically to relieve Job's boils by resorting to the same action that once brought boils upon others.

[21] See Job 42:7–8. Also see the Babylonian Talmud Tractate *Bava Metzia* 58b that brings the case of Job's friends as the epitome of insensitive discourse that is culpable for the pain it inflicts.

of empathy as well as the hyperbolically charged "throwing dust heaven-ward" also reflect the friends' subconscious resentment of Job's prior life of unmitigated wealth, reputation, religiosity, and family harmony. Could it be that on the level of conscious communication they are expressing empathy with his predicament, but subconsciously there is a measure of satisfaction with the burst bubble of Job's fairy-tale perfection?

We all certainly recognize the prevalent if unbecoming tendency of *Schadenfreude*, of feeling some small degree of satisfaction when the overly fortunate suffer misfortune. In the exaggeration, then, as well as in the intertextual reference, we find literary indicators of a subtext that deepens character portrayal by pointing to unconscious motivation.

On the level of surface communication between the friends and Job, what is happening is empathy and consolation. On the level of communication between the writer and the reader, it is precisely the rough edges of the text: the unconventional descriptive hyperbole, the odd choice of phrasing, and the importing and superimposing of another text—that enriches our characterization of these characters and our understanding of their relationship to each other. It is as if the writer speaks through the characters, yet (over their heads) directly to the reader with both a wink and with arrows pointing to parallel texts and to subtexts.

Through this example, we also mean to stress that in this mode of interpretation, the subconscious level revealed by the subtext is that of the portrayed literary character; it is not the presumed subconscious of the author.

A Word about Close Reading, Overinterpretation, and Bean Counting

One person's close reading is another's *overinterpretation*. This comment on the subjectivity inherent in all text interpretation is not to be seen as pertaining to the debate between pragmatists like Rorty (who see all interpretation as "use of texts") and the essentialists. The subjectivity we address should be associated with the approach of Umberto Eco and others who still believe that one can make distinctions between reading *out* of a text that which is potentially there and reading *into* a text something clearly external to it.[22]

While still far from the presumptuous posture of those who claim to have captured **the** meaning of a biblical passage, I do believe that one can still make the old distinctions between what the rabbinic tradition called *peshat* and that which they refer to as *derash.* One can still talk of various *meanings* of the text and not merely of *uses.* This brings me to an attempt to define what it is that guided me in these *close readings,* and why I often resort to what some readers might see as *bean counting* (when I provide statistical backing to the claim of the use of rare or anomalous wording).

If one is to claim that there is such a thing as artistic use of *wrong* wording or anomaly in a text, there must also be an inherent assumption as to the coherence or incoherence of that text. If attributing significance to what one perceives as anomalous in a verse will be more than a manipulative *use* of the text, one must be able to show by some quantitative measure that the wording is unusual in biblical usage. This is why I will often provide statistical backing to assertions that a phrase or word is being used in ways that are either unique or atypical in biblical writings.

Rather than reflecting a pedantic penchant for bean counting, these numbers provide the only possible support to the concept of a feigned slip of tongue or quill. Even the Viennese master would be hard pressed to grant significance to a man referring to his father as "farther" if the local dialect contained thirty percent of the population who would respond ingenuously to Freud, saying: "stop *borther*ing us about this; we all have perfectly fine *farthers.*"

---

[22] See note 9 and Eco's exchange of articles with Rorty in his book.

A Serious Word About Wordplay and the Idiosyncrasies of Orality

In some sections of this book, I employ a frequently neglected tool of literary analysis that is based on phonetic similarities between words as well as other forms of wordplay. We will contend that seeing these phenomena as purposeful (and artistic) writing is more than fanciful and should be taken quite seriously by close readers of the text. Support for this contention may be found in two contextual observations: the one—based on the density or prevalence of such wordplay (in the particular passages under scrutiny) compared to the less frequent use of word play in the rest of biblical writing; the other is based on a general observation that biblical style owes much of its peculiarity to the *oral-aural* nature of the written word that typifies the ancient Near East.

When one passage contains a verse that reads in the Hebrew, *hagida na shemekha* ("pray tell me your name" Gen. 32:30–32) and three verses later the unique phrase **gid hanashe** appears with what seems at first glance to be a totally disconnected meaning of "dislocated sinew [of the thigh]," one is justified in noting phonetic wordplay. Moreover, when in the same passage, several other phonetic "sound-alikes" and anagrams appear with a density that is highly unusual if not unique in the Bible, one is justified in moving past the mere noting of the phonetics to an attempt to explain what seems to be a conscious and artful use of it.

Though Genesis Chapter 32 has a particular literary reason to turn words inside out (as it is about wrestling and about the turning inside into outside of a biblical protagonist), it is also the case that the sounds of words, their musicality, and their phonetic resonance is a much overlooked aspect of biblical writing in general.

The modern rediscovery of the centrality of the dominant medium for any given cultural context has produced a rich literature in which McLuhan and his disciples and colleagues are but a notable few. Surely, one must attribute significance to the fact that historically the Hebrew biblical texts were written in an era in which all writings were experienced by their mass audiences exclusively through the aural sense. In fact, as long as written media were scrolls and early codices—as opposed to the mass-produced books of the print era—visual contact with this extraordinarily expensive medium remained inaccessible to any common person (as opposed to royalty, wealthy nobility and clergy). One can assume that the Bible was written for the entire people to study and live by its word (as is indicated by many internal passages). It is therefore apparent that the ancient scriptures were written primarily to be heard.

It is in this context that we may explain various attributes of the Hebrew language and of biblical style that are so foreign to the parochial understanding of moderns. Ancient Hebrew script has no vowels, they are provided vocally by the reader. When the ninth and tenth century Masoretes of Tiberius attached vowels and punctuation to the texts, it is of note that the same punctuation markings also serve as musical or cantillation signals.

Moreover, the phenomenon of the prevalent artistic use of *repetition* (and the subtle creation of expectation and the resulting nuance and surprise that ensue) is also directly related to the orality of ancient Hebrew scripture. The closest we moderns can come to an appreciation of a medium of writing that is experienced through the ear is to compare that writing to our experience of music. Just as musical meaning is conveyed through themes and variations on those themes, there is a musicality in the ancient written Hebrew that promotes the extensive and finely tuned use of repetition. I have found this to be true on many levels and have seen it manifest in a variety of artistic modes of repetition in the Bible.

These include: the repetition of verbatim phrases, in what Alter calls type-scenes, in what Buber and Rosenszeig called the repeated guiding word or *leitwort* (similar to the musical term, leitmotif), in the doubling and tripling of separate episodes, in the reporting of the same event through the slight variation of various perspectives, and in the pervasive use of parallelism in prose as well as poetry.

It is thus also probable that the use of phonetic wordplay, when evidenced in a given verse or section, is also a natural product and vehicle for the conveying of meaning or associative connection as well as for the evoking of pleasure, irony, surprise and a broad range of literary effect.

In short, what might be regarded as a fanciful conjecture as to the meaning of phonetic word play in modern writing, might be elevated to the status of *close reading* when the subject of analysis is the ancient era of "musical" writing for the ear.

Ultimately, the status of any suggestion that attributes meaning to wordplay, as is the case in any form of close reading, will be entirely dependent on the resonance and coherence of those suggestions with the specific context and with the literary work as a whole.

One more word about wordplay: Though a particular suggestion of artistic use of wordplay may find support in the common etymological history of two similar words, in no way is the historical commonality of word origin a *sine qua non* for the claim of interterxtual reference, or of words at play with each other. Derrida has called this kind of literary puns "syllepsis," a term that was previously used to denote a larger category of any word understood two different ways at once. In literary thought, words are taken as symbols with an indeterminate range of meaning and association. Then, along come context, syntax and grammar, and they constrict the readers' choice among the competing meanings. However, larger contexts of literary association—for instance, the other chapters of the same book or other books in the same canon—reintroduce additional meanings into the legitimate range of significance for the reader when the similarity between two words or phrases is unusual or striking. The probability increases that a word is being used to *connote* as well as to *denote*, when the word in context is anomalous, uncommon, or ungrammatical. To quote the critic, Michael Riffaterre:

"As I see it, ambiguity exemplifies the idiolectic ungrammaticalities that warn the reader of latent intertext."[23]

He goes on to speak of the duality of a text's message, its semantic and its semiotic faces. Riffaterre defines this phenomenon in the following way:

> "... syllepsis consists in the understanding of the same word in two different ways at once, as contextual meaning and as intertextual meaning. The contextual meaning is that demanded by the word's grammatical collocations, by the word's reference to other words in the text. The intertextual meaning is another meaning the word may possibly have, one of its dictionary meanings and/or one actualized within an intertext. In either case, this intertextual meaning is incompatible with the context and pointless within the text, but it still operates as a second reference—this one to the intertext. The second reference serves as a model for reading significance into the text... or as an index to the significance of straddling two texts."[24]

In any case, the use of wordplay as syllepsis—and as indicating the superimposition of one text's context upon the other—falls within a literary program that exists outside the boundaries of etymological analysis (though the latter may at times bolster the assertion of conscious wordplay).

---

[23] M. Riffaterre, "Syllespsis" in *Critical Inquiry, Vol. 6, Number 4* (Chicago: Univ. of Chicago, 1980) 628.
[24] Ibid., 637–8. (Also quoted in George Savran, "Beastly Speech: Intertextuality, Baalam's Ass and the Garden of Eden" in *Journal for the Study of the Old Testament 64* (1994).

Repetition, Repetition, Repetition

Repetition is one of the defining characteristics of biblical writing. Bible critics have based much of their documentary theory of multiple authors on the prevalence of repeated action, the doubling of episodes, and the appearance of nearly identical yet distinct passages. Echoing ancient Rabbinic exegesis and some medieval commentaries, modern literary exegetes have more recently argued that repetitions should be seen as literary tools that create themes and then proceed to produce nuance and complexity by providing variations on those themes. As noted, this is accomplished in much the same way that a musical composition works a theme to foster meaning.

But *repetition* is also one of the defining characteristics of inner compulsion (i.e., neurotic behavior) in psychoanalytic thinking. In the relentless effort to discover coherence in irrationality, the psychoanalytic lens is always on the lookout for patterns of behavior that reveal themselves through repetition. Even in the untrained intuitive observations of the layman, one often hears phrases like "I don't know why I *always* seem to. . . ." In this sense, repetition constitutes an unconscious need to work out unresolved issues, a need to redo that which was done poorly or incompletely.

There is yet an additional mode of repetition, closely related to the above, in which the reenacting of prior patterns can be redemptive. When *repetition* as reenacting is controlled and manipulated in the therapeutic context, it can also be the key to cathartic breakthrough. It is repetition artificially produced that allows compulsive behavior to free itself, by playing out the compulsive pattern before a mirror of self-reflection (the therapist)—thereby connecting the prior short circuit between unrecognized, unconscious motivations and heretofore inexplicable and often self-destructive behavior.

Philip Rieff, in describing Freud's understanding of the role of transference in therapy, had this to say about the emancipative power of repetition and of transference:

"Self-consciousness, to emancipate, needs another self, a sympathetic audience before which the unacted part of life can at last be acted out."[25]

To cure or curb the compulsion to repeat unhealthy emotional patterns, one grants the compulsion the "right to assert itself" in the controlled playground of transference.

The story of Jacob, similar to many other complex biblical narratives, is fraught with repetitions, cycles, and patterns of action and reaction. In our case, the hero repeatedly resorts to dubious means to achieve that which might have come his way without the subterfuge. At several junctures, Jacob's actions are perceived by his rivals as duplicitous and as a result, his initial goals recede even further from realization. Such a pattern occurs with the "lentil soup for birthright" barter, with the impersonation of Esau, and again with the speckled and spotted sheep arrangement with Laban. Are these to be understood purely as literary manipulations—there to entice the reader with the expectations created by thematic similarity and to surprise the reader with the variations on those themes that create nuance and depth? If it were so, this would be sufficient to warrant a sensitive reading of these passages as sophisticated literary art.

Nonetheless, the question that a psychologically oriented reader might ask is the following: Is the pattern just a result of the constrictions of behavior artificially imposed by the author upon the story's plot? Or is it the product of a much more subtle, inner compulsion that, in turn, derives from the uniqueness and psychological coherence of the literary character?

Indeed, we propose to explore this second possibility, namely, that the repetitions and patterns represent inner compulsions that are an essential part of developing Jacob's character as he struggles for autonomy and

---

[25] Philip Rieff, *Freud: The Mind of the Moralist* (Chicago: Univ. of Chicago, 1979) 169–170.

redemption. One of the literary phenomena that particularly astonished me as I moved through the Jacob stories with this perspective, was the following literary sequence: At the culmination of a repeated pattern of irrationally self-destructive manipulations, we find the previous scenes quite literally *reproduced* in the scene at the Jabok crossing. There, a symbolically instructive encounter occurs with a wrestling angelic figure playing the role of a "divine therapist." It is there that a controlled playground is provided in which Jacob can replay the prior moments with previously repressed awareness. It is there that he will achieve some integration (integrity?) of identity. The wrestling angel (of Genesis 32) not only renames Jacob, he also reframes his prior pattern of behavior. We shall see as well in our final essay that Moses too is confronted with a threatening divine messenger (Ex. 4) in a scene that contains idiosyncratic echoes of the prior scene with Jacob. There too, the scene is about Moses' internal struggle with his own compulsions that threaten to inhibit his ability to function as God's messenger.

I was surprised and gratified to find in these biblical narratives an artful use of repetition that approximates the psychological conception of repetition as unconscious reworking/compulsion as well as that of artificial reenactment functioning as therapeutic catharsis.

One of the defining characteristics of the narratives of the Hebrew Bible is its unflinchingly honest portrayal of its heroes as flawed, complex, and utterly human. At the same time, it is clear from the general framing of these narratives that they are not intended as phenomenological sketches, as "slice of life" portrayals devoid of ultimate mythic significance. The Bible decidedly does not conform to the schematic morality tales of contrived simplicity nor does it conform to the genre of ancient tales of heroism devoid of moral voice or theological pretension.

It therefore seems essential to inquire as to the implied lesson or purpose in describing the struggles, failings, conquests, and repeated failings of these protagonists. If the moral lessons of simply what to do and what not to do, or the record of interaction between human foible and divine plan were the sum total of the literary program, the repetitions and psychological complexity of the characters would seem at worst—a distraction, and at best—a literary embellishment. Yet, close readings of these stories betray increasingly intricate layers of artistic subtlety and purpose. Thus, it seems likely that the process itself of repeated struggle and failure, of empowerment and retreat, of self-estrangement and self-recognition, may just comprise a main thrust of this "divine anthropology."

A Word About the Question of Human Autonomy and Divine Authority

Ultimately, the questions raised here reverberate beyond the pages of the Bible and beyond the confines of any particular reading of Scripture. For any religious system of thought, one of the most central questions to be addressed will be: Can one develop an internalized, autonomous, moral compass and simultaneously, a deeply felt sense that one's own life and the grand scheme of history are guided by a transcendental, infinite force? Philosophical religious literature of both rational and mystical orientation grapples with this tension in proposing various theories of the parameters of divine providence and the scope of human free will. On the surface, the Hebrew Bible, in constructing an intricate and pervasive set of commandments and prophecies, has reduced the concern for human autonomy in deference to the call for submission to an external higher calling.

Debate persists on the extent of true autonomy or freedom for the individual. It is a common assumption that the ancients perceived one's life as circumscribed by the grand forces of nature and of the gods or God, whereas the moderns have shifted the focus to one's internal battle with the determinism of nature and nurture. However, I believe the Jacob stories, like much of the Hebrew Bible, bear strong evidence of a very early understanding of the powerful effects of internal circumscriptions or what we today would call neuroses. The struggles described in the book of Genesis are not primarily the struggles between kings and prophets, between nations, or even between brothers. They are, for the most part, the internal struggles of human beings to create destiny out of fate and to achieve an identity that is profoundly human, while at the same time, moving in harmony with and in pursuit of a divine vision or mandate.

The idea of the fulfillment of divine promise through human struggle, indeed, the very biblical idea of transcendence through actualization of the divine image within us, is a very tricky business. Can a human being transcend or even aspire to the divine without first being a fully autonomous person?

In C.S. Lewis' classic book, *The Screwtape Letters*, in which the veteran devil instructs his apprentice on the workings of "our father below" (Satan) and that of "the Enemy" (God), the devil argues the following:

> "To us a human is primarily food; our aim is the absorption of its will into ours, the increase of our own area of selfhood at its expense. But the obedience which the Enemy [God] demands is quite a different thing. One must face the fact that all the talk about His love for men, and His service being perfect freedom, is not... mere propaganda, but an appalling truth. He really *does* want to fill the universe with a lot of loathsome little replicas of himself —creatures whose life, on its miniature scale, will be qualitatively like His own, not because He has absorbed them but because their wills freely conform to His. We want cattle who can finally become food; He wants servants who can finally become sons. We want to suck in; He wants to give out.... Our war aim is a world in which our Father below has drawn all other beings into himself: the Enemy wants a world full of beings united to Him but distinct."[26]

---

[26] C.S. Lewis, *The Screwtape Letters* (London: The Guardian, 1961) Letter 8.

In his inimitably entertaining way, Lewis has made a most crucial distinction, and it is precisely with regard to this issue that the modern secularist view (as well as some religious fundamentalist views) got the Bible all wrong. In post-Freudian Western thought there is a bias toward religion in general and to the Hebrew Bible specifically that portrays them as conflicting with a humanistic vision of empowerment and autonomy. The idea of a deity conferring blessings and curses, issuing commands, and prefiguring history through prophetic visions, is seen as constricting the moral independence and powerful sense of self-mastery necessary for human fulfillment.

A close reading of various biblical texts, however, may reveal that the more dominant theme in the Hebrew Bible is that of a divinely inspired human autonomy and of an uncompromising demand from on high for human accountability. Ultimately, it is an invitation to "mere" mortals to transcend their self-imposed limits, to develop their innate divine image, to struggle with themselves, and even to "struggle with God. . . and to prevail."[27]

If a similarity between the psychoanalytic enterprise and the biblical narratives emerges from the texts themselves, it would seem to be found in the biblical hero's struggle to achieve identity and autonomy. This seems to occur, much as in the therapeutic model, by courageously confronting our own masquerades and evasions.

Moreover, what frankly came as a surprise to me—in the process of these close readings of the *Jacob* stories—was the extent to which the struggle for human autonomy could be traced precisely by reading between the lines, by noting trauma, resistance, cognitive dissonance, and repression, and by discerning compulsive repetition, slips of tongue, dreams as expressions of the unconscious, and the therapeutic effect of transference.

In short, the text itself describes the struggle for wholeness as being advanced (though not achieved) through a process remarkably similar to

---

[27] Gen. 32:29.

the essential dialectics of psychoanalysis.

If we are to learn about ourselves and are meant to read these tales of *"struggling with God and men"* as mirroring the struggle to become fully human and even to transcend our own humanity, then the narratives must, in turn, mirror the most subtle paradox of what it means to be inescapably human, yet endowed with the capacity for transcendence.

The successive chapters will deal with the internal struggles of biblical heroes: Isaac, Rebecca and Jacob, and Moses and Baalam. Their lives have been altered and challenged by a divine call and a covenantal destiny. They can no longer live simply on the plane of human action and reaction. Yet conversely, the biblical narrative does not exempt them from the consequences of their own motivations and moral decisions; they can deny or ignore neither their responsibility for their own lives nor their role in advancing or inhibiting the divine scheme.

Because of the nature of biblical narrative that consists of action and dialogue to the near exclusion of complex descriptive passages, the subtle indicators of internal struggle and psychological complexity in biblical protagonists can only be unpacked by means of close philological and literary analysis.

The following essays will employ the classical tools of paying close attention to anomalous language, grammar, syntax and sequence in the original biblical Hebrew. We will be especially attentive to the literary use of "intertextuality," in which borrowed phrases or constructs of plot are imported from text to text in order to point to the superimposition of one story upon the other. At the same time, we suggest that the relationship between text and subtext often mirrors the interplay of the conscious and the subconscious of biblical characters.

CHAPTER ONE

ISAAC'S ABRAHAM:
SHALL THE BLESSINGS OF THE FATHERS BE VISITED UPON THE SONS?

In examining the family of Isaac and Rebecca and their two sons Jacob and Esau, the towering figure of Isaac's father, Abraham, looms in the background. In fact, it will become clear that we cannot begin to analyze the unique dynamics of the family of Isaac and Rebecca until we ponder the previous generation's relationship between Abraham and Isaac.

This need to reflect back to Isaac as son of Abraham in order to understand Isaac as father to his own sons is highlighted by the text itself at the very beginning of this family's story:

> "These are the generations of Isaac son of Abraham: Abraham begat Isaac." (Gen. 25:19)

The passage then moves on to describe the barren Rebecca, Isaac's prayer, and the tumultuous pregnancy of twins during which God reveals to Rebecca the prophecy of two great nations that will emerge from her womb. But when we compare this introductory verse to similar verses that begin with the familiar coinage "these are the generations of," we are left not only with the redundancy of "Isaac son of Abraham: Abraham begat Isaac,"[1] but also with a break from the biblical convention of *"generations"* proceeding to describe subsequent progeny, **not** returning to previous ancestry.[2]

By confounding readers' expectations, the text has subtly pointed us toward understanding that the described relationships go beyond mere genealogy. Not only is Isaac biologically *generated* by Abraham, but the entire story of Isaac and his sons will be generated by the story of Isaac as son of Abraham. In other words, Isaac's relationship to his father is the contextual frame within which we understand what is to transpire with Jacob and Esau.

Having noted this, there can be no doubt as to the defining moment in the life of Isaac as son of Abraham. The near sacrifice—the *akeda*—of Isaac at the hands of his father on the mountaintop at Moriah explicitly informs the destiny of Abraham, who clearly emerges from the scene transformed and blessed by God (Gen. 22:16–19). But what of Isaac? How does he emerge from being bound and nearly sacrificed? Or more to the point, does he ever emerge and totally rejoin life? How did the *akeda* impact Isaac's subsequent relationship to his own sons?

Regarding these matters, the text speaks eloquently through poignant omission. The biblical narrative (Gen. 22:6, 8) repeats the phrase "the two of them *walked together*" at two distinct stages describing the ascent of Abraham and Isaac to Mount Moriah. The descent from the mountain, however, is described as "and Abraham returned to his boys [the servant

---

[1] Rashi, following Talmudic and Midrashic commentaries, sees the repetitive underscoring as an emphatic reassurance of Abraham's paternity as Sarah's brief captivity in the palace of Avimelech may have called this into question.

[2] "The generations of Isaac son of Abraham" should proceed immediately to Jacob and Esau, as in the case of Gen. 37:2, where the parallel verse states, "these are the generations of Jacob; Joseph at age seventeen. . . ." See also Gen. 11:10 and 11:27.

boys left behind in 22:5] and *they* [not Abraham and Isaac, but Abraham and the boys!] *walked together* to Be'er Sheba, and Abraham dwelt in Be'er Sheba." The narrative, as it were, leaves Isaac atop the mountain. Abraham rejoins life, *he* walks with others, *he* dwells in community with others. Isaac remains alone, as if still bound to the altar, with the image of his father holding the slaughtering knife above his head. The conferral of the divine blessing solely upon his father continues to resound in his ears—"because you have done this thing and have not spared your son, your only one, I [God] will surely bless you" (Gen. 22:16–17). The very next words of the story are "and *Abraham* returned."

Notably, when the command to sacrifice Isaac is given by God, Isaac is described as "your son, your only one, the one you love" (22:2), but immediately after raising the sacrificial knife (in 22:12), and again in verse 16, Isaac is described as "your son, your only one" without the additional "the one you love." A lasting covenant of mythic proportions has been struck between Abraham and the Lord, but the bond between father and son has simultaneously been eclipsed and the text speaks poignantly of this through two sets of three nearly parallel phrases—in the ascent and later in the descent from the mountain. In one case the text omits the return of Abraham *together* with Isaac, and in the other it omits the words, "the one you love."

Is it strange then to find in Genesis 25:28 a verse introducing Isaac and Rebecca's relationship with their sons that tells us that Isaac loves only one of his sons and that even the flow of this love is contingent upon an act of the son providing food for Isaac?

Moreover, is it not likely that the provision of burnt meat ("hunt") to the mouth of Isaac by Esau, serves to unblock the clogged arteries or pathways of love as it unconsciously returns Isaac to the moment of relief in the terror of his near sacrifice—namely, the substitution of the "ram in the thicket" for his own life?

Isaac, unlike Abraham, does not return from Moriah; he remains, alone. In fact, throughout the following two stories, Isaac is absent. He is not mentioned in the story of the death and burial of his mother Sarah. Even more strikingly, he is absent in the search for and courtship of his own wife, which is orchestrated by his father and executed by his father's servant. When we finally meet Isaac again, he is, of course, walking alone. He has returned from a place he apparently visits often. Verse 63 of Genesis 24 uses a unique phrase in biblical writing—"**ba mi'bo**," literally: "came from coming."[3] We find Isaac meditatively strolling in the field toward evening "coming from his coming from Be'er Lachai Ro'i."

What is the significance of Be'er Lachai Ro'i (literally translated by Everett Fox as the "well of the living-one who sees me")? Why does Isaac habitually go there? Moreover, in a prelude to the passage with which we began our analysis (Gen. 25:19), the verse "and it was after the death of Abraham, and the Lord blessed Isaac his son" ends with the unlikely words "... and Isaac dwelt *with* Be'er Lachai Ro'i" (Gen. 25:11). This last verse is of particular interest, as in the Hebrew Bible, people always dwell *in* a place, never *with* a place. Only Isaac dwells *with* a place, a place called Be'er Lachai Ro'i. To dwell *with* a place may certainly evoke a sense of preoccupation if not obsession with the symbolic meaning of that place for the dweller.[4] As we shall have occasion to note even more forcefully

---

[3] See Maurice Samuel, *Certain People Of The Book* (New York: Knopf, 1959) 142–145. Admittedly, several commentaries, including the 13th century Nachmanides, translate **mi'bo** as "from the vicinity of." The phrasing is nonetheless unique and might still be literally translated as I have, despite similarities to Genesis 10:19 and 30, 13:10, and 25:18, wherein the meaning is clearly, *the outskirts* or *vicinity of*.

[4] Nachmanides understood the odd phrase to mean that he *dwelt near* the scene of Be'er Lachai Ro'i and that the usual "dwelling in" is not used because it is not a village or community but rather a landmark in the desert. Rather than contradicting my understanding of the evocative meaning of "dwelling with" it may actually support the thrust of it as one must ask what kind of excessively contemplative man makes a private dwelling place of a desert landmark? (Nachmanides' understanding of עם—generally "with"—as *near* is also supported by twenty-one other instances in the Bible according to the Even Shoshan Concordance. Some of Even Shoshan's examples are debatable.)

later on, biblical geography is often psychological territory.

We do know the key to the meaning of Be'er Lachai Ro'i for Isaac as it is the place of God's revealing a well (**Be'er**) to Hagar, the runaway maid-servant to Sarah and concubine to Abraham. It is the scene of the first banishment of Isaac's half brother, Ishmael, in the womb of the pregnant Hagar. The second banishment of Hagar and Ishmael (Gen. 21) imme-diately precedes the binding of Isaac (Gen. 22). The banishment of the other sons of concubines (half brothers to Isaac) is told in Gen. 25:5–6: "Abraham gave all that he owned to Isaac, but to the sons of the concubines, Abraham gave gifts and sent them away from his son Isaac."

This latter verse is the next to last item of information we receive about Isaac just before the anomalous phrase "and Isaac dwelt *with Be'er Lachai Ro'i.*" It would seem that Be'er Lachai Ro'I, as psychological territory, rep-resents the unresolved trauma of the banishment of brothers. It represents the symbolic location of Sarah and Abraham's preference for Isaac to the extent of *sacrificing* the half-brothers for his sake.[5] As such, it serves as the locus for Isaac's contemplative attempts to absorb the willingness of his father to sacrifice other sons, and perhaps subliminally the even greater trauma of his father's readiness to sacrifice him. When confrontation with the deepest wound is not possible on a conscious level, it is displaced, simulated, and sometimes sublimated by immersion in (*dwelling with*) the next to worst, yet similar, trauma. Thus, we may have traced a route for the unreturned (unresolved?) Isaac atop Moriah who makes his way continu-ally to the site of Ishmael's banishment and dwells **with Be'er Lachai Ro'i** just prior to the birth of his own sons.

---

[5] Various writers have highlighted the striking similarities of theme and language linking Genesis 21, the banishment of Ishmael, with Genesis 22, the binding of Isaac. Both stories begin with "Abraham rose early in the morning" and reach their climax with "and an angel of the Lord called out from the heavens." Some commentaries even refer to the banishment of Ishmael as "the little akeda." My reading here carries the comparison still further and may account for the underlying meaning of the purposeful literary patterning that connects the two chapters.

We may also have accounted for the odd juxtaposition of the two parts of the verse (Gen. 25:11) that states, "after the death of Abraham, *God* blessed his son, Isaac—**and** Isaac dwelt with Be'er Lachai Ro'i." Precisely because of the juxtaposition of the death of Abraham with God's blessing of Isaac, Rashi (the prodigious 11ᵗʰ century commentator) notes that unlike Isaac and Jacob, Abraham does not bless his son.[6] It is likely then that Isaac dwells with an unfulfilled desire for the blessing of Abraham, or alternatively, an unconfirmed entitlement to the blessing of his father. This is so, additionally, because he neither descends from Moriah walking together with his father nor does he accept with equanimity the disenfranchisement of Ishmael (symbolized by Be'er Lachai Ro'i), nor the banishment of his other half brothers.

Indeed, when Isaac himself finally confers a blessing upon Jacob as Jacob (and not upon the son masquerading as Esau), the blessing is, tellingly, not "the blessing of Isaac," but the long awaited "blessing of Abraham" (Gen. 28:4). Ironically, Isaac should be giving his own blessing to Jacob, but he cannot bless him as Isaac, but rather only as Abraham. Isaac confers the "blessing of Abraham," that (paradoxically) he did not receive. Compounding the irony, in the first scene in which Isaac blesses Jacob, Isaac *does* bless as Isaac, but Jacob for his part, receives the blessing as Esau. The transmitting of generational legacy has short-circuited, and the phenomenon expresses itself through the signal of blessings, near blessings, and misdirected blessings.

Never having entirely returned from his near death at the hands of his father, Isaac can never experience the security of the unconditional love of Abraham. Thus, it is the Isaac *generated* by Abraham whom we meet in Genesis 25. His wife Rebecca bears twin boys who are loved differentially

---

[6] See Rashi's source Tanchuma (ed. Buber) *Lech Lecha* 5. It is noteworthy that an entire chapter (Genesis 27) is dedicated to the blessing Isaac gives his sons. Another chapter (Genesis 49) is dedicated to the blessing Jacob gives his sons. Only Abraham fails to bless Isaac; hence the additional weight that must be placed upon this verse: "and it was after the death of Abraham and *God* blessed Isaac his son."

by their parents and whose struggle for entitlement to blessings begins even in the womb. It is the lonely, bound, and nearly sacrificed Isaac who begets Jacob and Esau. The complex paternal character of these struggling brothers is himself the sibling of banished half brothers who dwells with Be'er Lachai Ro'i, and it is this Isaac who now desperately tries to find reasons to love the "wrong" son.

Again, irony runs deep, as we shall see. Isaac's attempts to compensate with love (brought on by the artificial stimulus of the providing of food), in order to keep within the family the sibling most likely to be the candidate for banishment, results in the banishment of the other brother. It will be Rebecca's failure to interpret correctly Isaac's preference for Esau that will lead her to induce Jacob to deception, and it is the deception that leads directly to Jacob's need to flee for his life. Moreover, Esau will also eventually leave the family in any case, and the son whom Isaac so desired to save from the fate of his own brother—the banished Ishmael—will join Ishmael and marry his daughter (Gen. 28:9).[7]

It is entirely in keeping with the psychological coherence of the narrative to conclude that a shattered integration of self (the very definition of trauma), or in other words, an experience so overwhelming as to have *bound* Isaac to the altar, has prevented him from returning to life with his father, and has informed Isaac's future identity as father to his own sons.

It is equally likely that a sense of *non-entitlement* preoccupies Isaac, the lonely half-brother of banished siblings, himself never blessed by his father. He will inevitably communicate this ambivalence of entitlement to his son Jacob, who, as we shall see, continually rejects the straight and direct route to entitlement (first vis-a-vis Esau and later with regard to Laban and his sons) opting for circuitous and questionable means to receiving reward

---

[7] The text highlights this irony by placing this verse (describing Ishmael's marriage to the paternal uncle-Ishmael's family), immediately prior to the forced departure of Jacob to the maternal uncle, Laban.

or blessing. Indeed, the "history" *(toledot)* of Isaac as son of Abraham *generates* the history of Jacob, son of Isaac.

Moreover, there will be clear resonance to the previous stories of Isaac as son of Abraham when (in Genesis 27) the elderly Isaac—emotionally still bound to the altar of Moriah—will experience once more his own impending death and will contemplate the conferral of God's blessing upon one son at the expense of the other. It is there that he will return once again to the moment of relief (the substitution of the "ram in the thicket"), in ordering the killing of an animal and arranging for the smell of burnt meat to fill his nostrils once more. Is not this the meaning of the ancient midrash that explains the origin of Isaac's blindness at the time of blessing Jacob as the result of the stinging angelic tears that fell into his eyes while bound to the altar at Moriah? That is to say, Isaac—as father—is blind to (i.e., unable to distinguish between) his sons and this blindness is directly connected to the trauma of almost being sacrificed by his own father.[8] Is it coincidental that in contrast with Abraham and Jacob, who both bring animal sacrifices to God, Isaac never lifts the sacrificial knife, but only builds an altar?[9]

---

[8] See *Bereishit Rabba* (ed. Vilna) 65.
[9] Gen. 26:25.

CHAPTER TWO

CONDITIONAL LOVE AND
THE PURCHASE OF BIRTHRIGHT

Our story moves on to relate the birth of twins to Rebecca and Isaac. Already in the womb, there is a struggle between them, and Rebecca receives the prophetic pronouncement, "two peoples are in your belly, and two nations from your intestines shall diverge, and each nation shall outdo the other and the older shall serve the younger."[1] The first is born a hairy and ruddy child, and is named Esau—עשׂו, related etymologically to the

---

[1] It should be noted that according to both R. David Kimche (Radak, 13th cent.) and R. Joseph Ibn Caspi (13th cent.), biblical Hebraic syntax allows a reading of the last phrase that sees "the older" as object instead of subject, in which case the phrase may be read, "the older—the younger will serve." (For an additional example of such syntax, see Job 14:19.) The resulting ambiguity might be intended to enlist the reader's own ambivalence or to foreshadow the ambivalence of Isaac and Jacob. Interestingly, the only non-ambivalent character with regard to the intended recipient of the divine blessing is the only direct recipient of the prophecy, Rebecca. Nonetheless, readers will be aware of the possible secondary reading, and it will influence the tension, suspense and perhaps even the ultimate understanding of the outcome of the struggle. Whether one sees an ambiguity in syntax here will influence a reading that either presages an unequivocal fated destiny or a dialectic and conditional destiny for the descendants of Jacob and Esau.

Arabic cognate meaning *covering*, and possibly at play later in the text with the Hebrew root meaning *action*—עשה. The second emerges grasping the heel of his brother and is named Jacob—יעקב, etymologically related to **akeb**—עקב, meaning *heel*, and alternatively to words that mean *crooked*[2] or *to supplant* or *usurp* or to *come from behind*.[3] We begin the next part of our reading with Genesis 25, verses 27–34:

כז) וַיִּגְדְּלוּ הַנְּעָרִים וַיְהִי עֵשָׂו אִישׁ יֹדֵעַ צַיִד אִישׁ שָׂדֶה וְיַעֲקֹב אִישׁ תָּם יֹשֵׁב אֹהָלִים

כח) וַיֶּאֱהַב יִצְחָק אֶת עֵשָׂו כִּי צַיִד בְּפִיו וְרִבְקָה אֹהֶבֶת אֶת יַעֲקֹב

כט) וַיָּזֶד יַעֲקֹב נָזִיד וַיָּבֹא עֵשָׂו מִן הַשָּׂדֶה וְהוּא עָיֵף

ל) וַיֹּאמֶר עֵשָׂו אֶל יַעֲקֹב הַלְעִיטֵנִי נָא מִן הָאָדֹם הָאָדֹם הַזֶּה כִּי עָיֵף אָנֹכִי עַל כֵּן קָרָא שְׁמוֹ אֱדוֹם

לא) וַיֹּאמֶר יַעֲקֹב מִכְרָה כַיּוֹם אֶת בְּכֹרָתְךָ לִי

לב) וַיֹּאמֶר עֵשָׂו הִנֵּה אָנֹכִי הוֹלֵךְ לָמוּת וְלָמָּה זֶּה לִי בְּכֹרָה

לג) וַיֹּאמֶר יַעֲקֹב הִשָּׁבְעָה לִּי כַּיּוֹם וַיִּשָּׁבַע לוֹ וַיִּמְכֹּר אֶת בְּכֹרָתוֹ לְיַעֲקֹב

לד) וְיַעֲקֹב נָתַן לְעֵשָׂו לֶחֶם וּנְזִיד עֲדָשִׁים וַיֹּאכַל וַיֵּשְׁתְּ וַיָּקָם וַיֵּלַךְ וַיִּבֶז עֵשָׂו אֶת הַבְּכֹרָה

27) "And the lads grew and Esau became a man knowing hunt, a man of the field—and Jacob—a simple man, a dweller of tents.
28) And Isaac loved Esau because of the hunt [venison] in his mouth;[4] but Rebecca loves Jacob.

---

[2] See particularly Jeremiah 9:3, which will be referred to later, and Isaiah 40:4.

[3] See Harold Fisch's translation of Genesis 27:36 *The Jerusalem Bible* (Jerusalem: Koren, 1969).

[4] Commentaries have pointed out that the possessive "his" in "the hunt in **his** mouth" referring to Isaac's penchant for venison, could alternatively refer to Esau, particularly if the word hunt is to be understood as a synonym for guile or cunning. In this reading, Isaac's love for Esau is attributed to Esau's ability to deceive his father with guileful words. Though this improbable secondary meaning is possible, the irony would be that Esau in context seems anything but guileful, as both with Jacob

29) And Jacob concocted a stew and Esau came from the field and he was famished.

30) And Esau said to Jacob: "Please give me of that red, red stuff to gulp down, for I am faint" and therefore his name was called **Edom** [Red].

31) And Jacob said: Sell to me as of today your birthright [literally: primogeniture]."

32) And Esau said, "Behold I am about to die, what need have I of birthrights."

33) And Jacob said, "Swear to me as of today," and he swore to him and he sold his birthright to Jacob.

34) And Jacob gave to Esau bread and lentil stew and he ate and drank and rose and left and *disdained* the birthright.

As readers we know the end of the story, and so, as we read in these verses the background to that which will occur, we search for origin, for causation, and at the very least for early intimations of the later development of character and plot. How does a family reach the depths of dysfunction in which a wife enlists her son's compliance in deceiving her blind husband (his father) in order to rob her own son (his brother) of his blessing? What forces of miscommunication are already germinating that will eventually bear the fruits of hate, threatened fratricide, and the forced exile of a son from his loving mother?

The text, indeed, provides scant, yet telling, background: an agitated pregnancy, a maternal prayer and a prophetic promise, and a struggle of twins in the womb as to who shall emerge first. With the multiple birth, two different modes of negotiating life emerge: that of the hunter and that of the dweller of tents. Most significantly, we have what we are told and

---

and later with his father, he is scarcely capable of containing his emotions or urges let alone disguising them. In contrast, Jacob the *simple* dweller of tents, is portrayed as a schemer and as an actor capable of elaborate deception.

what we are strikingly not told about the relationship between parents and sons.

In verse 28, the asymmetry is poetic and painful, as each of the two parents loves only one child. The father's love is conditional, based on a ritual between father and son involving the provision of food; the mother's love is unconditional (yet directed to one son exclusively). The 16th century author of the commentary, **Kli Yakar** (Rabbi Ephraim of Lonshitz), has also noted the asymmetry of verb tense, Isaac *loved* ויאהב, whereas Rebecca *loves* אהבת, implying that the love that is conditional is also situational and that only the unconditional love is continuous and abiding. Is the silence with regard to Isaac's affection for Jacob indicative of what he feels or of what he is capable of communicating? Perhaps the reader is being made to hear the silence that the sons hear. We are made to experience a fraction of the anxiety and doubt of Jacob and Esau.

Let us focus on Jacob. He experiences love, but only the love of a mother, a mother with a prophetic vision who will later reveal herself as an overbearing and managerial parent. He is deprived of the natural flow of his father's love, a love that Esau only manages to receive by the artificial means of supplying venison.

Conventional psychological insight often sees the ongoing love of the mother figure as an encompassing love that totally embraces the child as an indistinguishable part of herself, as indeed the child in the womb once was. The father figure sees the child as a separate entity that will be bound to him by the love that the child will earn and deserve. This dichotomy is too simplistic and generally subject to the particular constellations of greatly differing family dynamics. Yet in this case, the text seems to support the cliche to a greater extent than one would have expected.

Rebecca will dress her adult son (27:15–16) and will instruct him to follow her unquestioningly (Gen. 27:8, 13). She will comfort him with the impossible assertion that the consequences of *his* actions will fall only upon *her* (Gen. 27:13). Perhaps it is precisely the unconditional, and all-embracing, character of her love (of classic maternal love in general?) that leaves Jacob with what we shall discern as a persistent sense of lack of entitlement. It is a love that is based on Rebecca's vision (a vision that came to her while pregnant and a love that sees Jacob as an extension of her own sovereign self, even post-partum and well into his adulthood). It is not a love that is dependent upon or reflective of Jacob's fulfillment of his autonomous self. It is therefore a love that leaves him hungry and desperate for another kind of love, for the blessing of a father who seems to love only Esau. Jacob becomes dependent on the love of mother, precisely because of the absence of evidence of his father's love, an irony analogous to that of the child who should be weaned, but continues to seek sustenance from that which can no longer nourish him.[5] Mother's love must compensate for the much desired but unattainable love of father, yet it is uniquely unsuited for the task.[6]

The text, with its literary payload of artistic asymmetry, thus sets the scene for the developments of Chapter 27. There, Jacob, who lacks a sense of self-mastery, will relinquish his moral autonomy to the mother on whom he depends for love, in order to attain the very object of his desperation—father's love or blessing.

To gain an understanding of the struggle for blessing/birthright,[7] and

---

[5] We will play on this imagery later in discussing the anomalous mention of the death of Rebecca's nursemaid, Devorah, who accompanies Jacob through his exile and return from Laban's house.

[6] Despite wariness of an artificial application of classic Freudian categories even for the sake of contrast to my own reading of the text, I cannot help but note that there seems to be a partial reversal here of the Oedipal idea. If our claim is indeed supported by the storyline, the father's love is the goal of the child, and mother proves to be an obstacle. Of course, my suggestion is, in fact, more complex than this as I understand the child's needs as incorporating both the father and mother modes of love. See Erich Fromm, *The Art of Loving* (NY: Harper and Row, 1974) 36–44.

[7] The words in Hebrew for these two distinct but related concepts is almost the same, involving only the switched order of two letters—ברכה and בכרה (*berakha and bekhora*). Is this not perhaps a clever manipulation of form and content, as the story at hand is that of *switching the order of two*, in the conferral of blessing and

of the later deception scene, we will need to study the introductory scene of the lentil soup. Yet, returning momentarily to Isaac, we are reminded of the possibility that the lonely, contemplative Isaac, whose father's hand is still outstretched above the altar, is afraid or incapable of communicating his affection for Jacob. Isaac's love, which appears to be stimulated only by situational ritual, is directed instead to the more likely candidate for banishment[8]—not to Jacob the probable inheritor of "Abraham's blessing," but to Esau, the Ishmael-like character and the potential bearer of the legacy of Be'er Lachai Ro'i. And as we have suggested, it is not coincidence that the situational ritual that arouses his love involves the smell of burnt meat, harking back to the moment of relief at Moriah, with the staying of Abraham's hand and the substitution of burnt meat for his own fragile life.

But back to lentils and to Jacob. How to earn Isaac's blessing? Can one really purchase a birthright through the sale of a brother's broth? Can the exploitation of his brother's vulnerability, of this ruddy hunter's need for immediate gratification, really provide Jacob with a true sense of entitlement or with a confirmation of his father's love or blessing? And if not, is there not something movingly pathetic about the attempt of the unloved son to win his father's recognition through dubious purchase?

The 19th century commentary **Ohr Hachaim** (Rabbi Chaim Ibn Attar) addresses this issue as he astutely interprets the juxtaposition of verse 28 (Isaac's love of the ruddy Esau on account of food) to verse 29 (Jacob

---

birthright? The switching of the order of letters subtly reflects and underscores the switching of the order of sons. This mechanism (of the symbolic substitution of two closely related items or concepts reflected by the reversal of two letters that distinguish the words from each other) may also be present later in the story with regard to *minha* and *mahaneh* —מחנה - מנחה, and still more subtly with *gedi* and *gid*, גדי - גיד. My thanks go to former student Elisheva Shulman for pointing out the latter.

[8] Esau is described as "a man of the hunt, a man of the field" in terms very similar to the prior description of Ishmael (the banished brother of Isaac) who is described as "a man of the wild, his hand upon all and all hands upon him" (Gen. 16:12).

cooking a meal of red, thick stew):

> "Perhaps as he saw that Esau's feeding of Isaac was effective [in producing love] he also pursued the path of cooking a meal in order to bring closer his father's heart, as had Esau."[9]

Both the New Jewish Publication Society and the Schocken (Everett Fox) translations of these verses apparently sensed a non sequitur in the sequence of verses 28 and 29, as did Rashi. For them, there is no immediately discernible connection between the differential love of the two parents for the two sons and the subsequent cooking of lentil soup. Rashi suggests that the soup was a traditional mourning dish and is related to the death of Abraham that was reported in 25:8, twenty verses earlier. The NJPS and Schocken translations accept the perceived non sequitur, and therefore provide a transitional phrase to introduce a new scene by translating the beginning of verse 28, "Once when Jacob was cooking. . . ." There is no justification in the original Hebrew for adding the words *"Once when"* to the translation. Moreover, in light of Ohr Hachaim's observation, they have done a disservice to the English reader by smoothing out this bump in the reading.

By contrast, the KJV translation preserves the literal meaning and the apparent disconnect between the love for Esau (on account of food provided) but not for Jacob in verse 28, and the cooking of lentil soup in verse 29 by simply reading, "And Jacob sod pottage. . . ." This translation has left open a path for the English reader to more readily note the missing synapse and to appreciate the clever but convincing suggestion of Ohr Hachaim. The text has juxtaposed the absence of Isaac's love for Jacob (and the love for Esau on account of food) with Jacob's cooking a stew, in order to subtly indicate Jacob's motivation.

For Ohr Hachaim then, the background of the "lentil soup scene" is

---

[9] *Mikraot Gedolot, Ohr Hachaim,* s.v. *"vayazed,"* Gen. 25:29.

Jacob's desire for his father's love, even before the arrival of the famished Esau. It seems that the closest to providing red meat (venison) for Isaac that the smooth-skinned dweller of tents can attain and provide is to prepare a thick, vegetarian soup described by Esau as that "red, red stuff." Notably, the extension of this reading suggests yet another connection between the scene of the purchase of the birthright (the exploitation of Esau's hunger) and the deception of Isaac (the exploitation of Isaac's blindness).[10] The two episodes are connected by the anguished cry of Esau, "Is not he rightly called Jacob (usurper), for he has usurped me twice; he has taken my birthright and now he has taken my blessing."[11] Moreover, one may say that the first scene both parallels and foreshadows the second, as they both consist of *Jacob being Esau* in order to procure their father's love or preference.[12]

In light of this insight of Ibn Attar, we are also provided with an ad-

---

[10] Interestingly, the Talmud expands the category of forbidden behavior that violates the prohibition "... Thou shalt not put a stumbling block before the blind" (Lev. 19:14) to include all exploitation of the other person's handicap, weakness **or impulsivity**. One of the examples given is that of holding out a cup of wine to a nazirite (the equivalent of serving alcohol at a meal attended by a recovering alcoholic). See Babylonian Talmud Tractate *Pesachim* 22b.

[11] Gen. 27:36.

[12] There is additional indication of the connection between the barter of birthright for broth and the deceitful taking of Esau's blessing as well as an indication that the narration views both as exploitation for which a price must later be paid. In both stories there is an unusual word or phrase used to link this story to the future exploitation of the seed of Jacob at the hands of the children of Esau.

In Gen. 36:10–12 we are told that the grandson of Esau is Amalek, later to become a nation infamous in its persecution of the Israelites. Only thrice does the term *ayef* (famished) appear in the five books of Moses—twice describing Esau in the lentil soup scene and again in describing the weariness of Israelites in the desert when they are attacked by Amalekites. Furthermore, with regard to the anguish of Esau in the aftermath of Jacob's deceit with the blessings, the narration relates (Gen. 27:34) that Esau "**cried out a very great and bitter cry.**" The only other place in the Hebrew Bible where this phrase appears is in the book of Esther (4:1) where Mordekhai the Jew "**cries out a great and bitter cry**" because of the plot against his people on the part of Haman the Aggagite (Amalekite).

ditional layer of meaning to the literary parallel noted by Yair Zakovitch between the barter of lentil soup for birthright here and the barter of mandrakes for a conjugal night with Jacob (Gen. 30:14–18).[13] The two cases seem to be the only biblical instances of the barter of a perishable item (soup or flowers) for a legal or quasi-legal entitlement (priority of inheritance or of conjugal rights). Zakovitch suggests that the parallel between the two episodes may be part of a larger pattern of poetic justice that attends the stories of Jacob. Jacob, who exploits his brother's impulsive need for the soup in suggesting the barter, later becomes himself an object of the barter between Rachel and Leah. Zakovitch also notes that in both stories the phrase "And he came in from the field" is used—first in the lentil soup scene with regard to Esau and later in the *Dudaim* (mandrakes) scene in reference to Jacob. Zakovitch does not note in his comments that these are the only two verses in the entire Hebrew Bible that describe a single person as "coming from the field—ויבא...מן השדה." The uniqueness of the phrase goes even further in establishing Zakovitch's thesis of the purposeful paralleling by the text of these two stories. Moreover, one might suggest that poetic justice and the reversal of situations characterizes the two barter stories in yet another sense. Just as Jacob has usurped the "*ish yode'a tzayid*" (Esau was a **man who knew hunting [venison]**—Gen. 25:27) in competing with his *nezid* (lentil soup), and later by actually bringing a goat disguised as venison, so too, in the transition between chapters 25 and 30, Jacob has unwittingly become the "*ish sadeh*" (**man of the field**—also a prior description of Esau in the very same verse, Gen. 25:27). Jacob, it seems, is no longer the *ish tam, yoshev ohalim;*[14] by assuming the identity of Esau, he has become the *ish yode'a tzayid* and the *ish sadeh*.

Yet the parallel runs even deeper if one sees the lentil soup as an at-

---

[13] See Yair Zakovitch, *Mikraot Be'eretz Ha-mar'ot—Through the Looking Glass: Reflection Stories in the Bible* (Tel Aviv: Hakibbutz HaMeuchad, 1995) 16–17.

[14] See Gen. 25: 27, the translation: "a simple [or straightforward] man, a dweller of tents." In fact, it is this transformation that forces Jacob out of the protective tent of Rebecca and sends him into the exile with his treacherous Uncle Laban.

tempt to win Isaac's love. To begin with, the background to the barter of mandrakes in chapter thirty is also the pain of two siblings, one loved and one unloved, described in 29:30–31:

> "He [Jacob] loved Rachel more than Leah... and when God saw that Leah was [felt?] hated, He opened her womb, but Rachel was barren."

The fascinating discrepancy between the first half of this verse (Jacob loved Leah less than Rachel) and the second half (God saw that Leah was hated) is an intentional equating of unequal terms. The core of both this story and other stories of tragic sibling rivalry in the Bible, including the Jacob-Esau story and the Cain-Abel story, is that the "less loved" inevitably feels rejected or "hated." When this verse chooses not to highlight the psychological equation of the two by saying that *Leah* saw that she was hated, but rather that "*God* saw that she was hated," the text has heavy-handedly condemned the phenomenon of differential love.[15]

The biblical text continues to play out the theme of the anxiety of the less loved—as the first born of this unloved sibling (Leah), is called **Reuven**. His very name is explained to mean "for God has *seen* [Hebrew: **Ra'ah = Re'u**] [i.e., identified with] my affliction, in that now *my husband will love me*" (29:32). The child that is born to provide (and named after) the incentive or pretext for a love that is not forthcoming, Reuven, is next encountered picking mandrakes (considered to be an aphrodisiac or fertility herb) and bringing them to his mother. The Hebrew for mandrakes, דודאים *(dudaim)*, suggests the biblical term דוד *(dod)*—"beloved."[16] Hence one might be tempted to translate Reuven bringing "beloveds" to his

---

[15] This, despite the fact that in the Cain-Abel story it seems to be God himself who plays the role of the "parent" who accepts one child's offering and not the other. Interestingly, in that story as well, the accepted gift is the animal sacrifice (here, venison) and the unsuccessful effort is vegetarian (here, lentils).

[16] See also Song of Songs 7:14.

unloved (or less-loved) mother. When the impulsive Rachel asks for the flowers, Leah responds (equating the two), "is it not enough your taking of my man, will you also take my son's mandrakes?" Rachel offers the evening's conjugal rights that should have gone to her and in return Leah gives her the mandrakes.[17]

In light of this, we return to the unloved sibling Jacob who sees the love of Isaac for Esau and "understands" that the provision of food is a pretext or incentive for love that does not come his way. He cooks up a pot of soup in the hopes of getting that love. Similar to the case with Leah and the mandrakes, Jacob is then approached by the loved sibling who requests the object (after having already acquired the love). The response in both episodes is for the sibling who needs the object in order to obtain love, to barter the object in exchange for a more direct and tangible expression of preference. The birthright is the symbol and expression of father's love and preference, just as Leah's night with Jacob is the key to and reward of their husband's preference and love.

In both episodes, there is a less-loved sibling so desperate to obtain the affection of a third party, as to think that a material object might help them procure that love. When approached by the more-loved sibling who requests the material object, the deal is struck by trading the object for a more direct route to the receipt of that which the object was supposed to provide. In both scenes, the desperation of the unloved and the skewed perception of the relationship between objects and human attachments are underscored. Ohr Hachaim's interpretation paves the way for the

---

[17] Most probably, the unloved Leah sees the flowers as aphrodisiacs whereas the barren Rachel "needs" them as a fertility herb. Ironically, the result of the barter and that evening's cohabitation of Jacob with Leah is the pregnancy of Leah, and the later birth of Yissachar—יששכר (Hebrew: "**there is recompense**"). Perhaps there is partial recompense for Leah, but not as yet for the barrren Rachel, whose mandrakes have wilted as Leah's womb grows. However, in the prophetic vision of Jeremiah 31:14-15, the eschatological figure of Rachel the mother is comforted with the words," Keep your voice from weeping and your eyes from tears because for your labor **there is recompense**—"**יש שכר לפעולתך**".

more significant literary parallel between the stories, just as, reciprocally, the resulting intricately precise parallel lends further credence to both his insight and to that of Zakovitch:

Genesis 25:28–34	Genesis 29:30–30:18
Isaac (the father) bestows differential love to his two sons	Jacob (the husband) bestows differential love to his two wives (who are siblings)
Esau: the loved sibling	Rachel: the loved sibling
Jacob: the *less loved* sibling	Leah: the *less loved* sibling
Nezid adashim (lentil soup) cooked up by the less loved in poignant, if pathetically desperate, attempt to obtain Isaac's love	*Dudaim* (mandrakes) gathered on behalf of the less loved in poignant, if pathetically desperate, attempt to obtain Jacob's love
The *more loved* sibling asks the *less loved* for the object ("Pray feed me of that red, red stuff. . . .") 25:30	The *more loved* sibling asks the *less loved* for the object ("pray give to me of the mandrakes of your son") 30:14
Less loved sibling responds: if you want the object that was to gain for me father's preference—give me the preference itself (i.e., the birthright) 25:31	Less loved sibling responds: would you take from me the object that was to gain for me my husband's love as well as the love itself?! 30:15
Siblings arrive at a mutually agreed upon barter of an object (the soup) for an entitlement that more directly represents Isaac's love or preference —i.e., the birthright	Siblings arrive at a mutually agreed upon barter of an object (the mandrake flowers) for an entitlement that more directly represents Jacob's love or preference—i.e., the evening's conjugal rights
A bitter and ironic result to the barter: Jacob's recognition by his father as the preferred son does not occur, inner sense of entitlement for Jacob further recedes—sibling strife increases.	A bitter and ironic result to the barter: Leah the *less loved* remains less loved but becomes pregnant. The *more loved* Rachel remains barren. Sibling strife only increases.

Moreover, there is yet another literary indication that Ohr Hachaim was correct in understanding Jacob's desire to gain father's preference as a plan that preceded the arrival of Esau. (This same indicator will imply as well that the narrative voice does not view Jacob's exploitative behavior with moral neutrality.) In verse 29, the verb ויזד which I have translated as "concoct," involves an anomalous use of the root (z,i,d)—זיד, clearly at play with the similar word for stew נזיד **nezid**. This word in verb form, however, only appears ten times in the entire Hebrew Bible and in nine of those appearances the meaning is [to act with] malice aforethought (related to the oft-used term מזיד **mezid**, which also means "of malicious intent").[18] Surely the choice of verb here goes beyond the wordplay with **nezid** for stew, and through intertextual reference, points to the narration's view of this scene as even worse than the opportunistic exploitation that already offends the reader's sense of fair play.

While the last verse of the episode ("And Esau **spurned** the birthright" 25:34) makes clear that Jacob has taken from his brother only that which Esau was not capable of appreciating to begin with, we are still disturbed by Jacob's mode of achieving the result.[19] The sale of the birthright at the end of the episode remains a formal sale, replete with Esau's oath, but the

---

[18] For example, see Deuteronomy 18: 20. Most notably, see Exodus 21:13–14: "ואשר לא צ דה...וכי י ז ד". Here, the two terms *z-w-d* and *tz-d-h* come so close together in meaning and in proximity as to be used interchangeably. The verb for "to hunt "is used in the sense of "to stalk" and the verb for acting maliciously is used as "to plot." Hence, the two verses juxtapose the case of one killed by accident—אשר לא צדה (literally: has not been stalked) with the one murdered with malicious forethought—כי יזיד איש. This interchangeable use further confirms Ohr Hachaim's and our own comparison of Esau's ציד (hunt) and Jacob's ויזד נזיד (brewing a stew). Note as well the similar phonetics of z-d and tz-d; the letters ("z") ז and ("tz") צ are sometimes interchangeable as in the words זעק and צעק—"to cry out," and "to shout."

[19] Further irony and at the same time further psychological coherence are indicated by Esau's readiness to forfeit the birthright for such trivial and short-lived benefit. Just as Esau receives his father's preference by merely providing food (Gen. 25:28), he is willing to sell his father's preference for the mere receiving of food.

moral residue is still dripping from the bottom of the pot. The sense one gets is that of two brothers vying for the title of "most unsuitable for the birthright." In any case, we have seen the beginning of a pattern for Jacob, who will continually end up possessing that which he was intended to receive, but accomplishing it in a manner that calls that very entitlement into question. He will achieve things through his *Jacobness,* through attributes inherent in the name that also means "come from behind," "crooked," or what the translator Everett Fox playfully calls "heel-sneak."[20]

The irony of objects replacing or representing or procuring love is indicative of a larger theme at play in the Jacob stories. There is psychological resonance to the idea that an alienated identity, a lack of integration of self, will lead to a situation in which things substitute for emotions, children substitute for a core sense of being,[21] and brother masquerades as brother. As has been noted by Erich Fromm in *To Have Or To Be,* as well as by others, when an anchored sense of self, a secure identity in the mode of "being" is absent, one often witnesses the confusion of "having" for "being." Paradoxically, living in the mode of "having" as an artificial compensation for a fragile sense of "being" can only further exacerbate one's insecurity, as what I am—my identity—if defined by what I *have,* can also be lost or taken away.[22] In order to overcome this neurosis—a syndrome that expresses itself as a lack of mastery of one's own life—one must be grounded in a secure identity by a love that is not only the unconditional love of belonging to someone else, but also through the love that

---

[20] See Everett Fox, *The Five Books of Moses* (NY: Schocken, 1983) 155.

[21] Rachel tells Jacob "give me children or I am dead" (30:1). Ironically, she eventually dies in childbirth. Leah names her child, "now my husband will love me" (Gen. 29:32). Incidentally, yet a further parallel between the two "loved" siblings—Esau and Rachel—is embedded in the impulsive and dramatic language they use to describe their predicaments. Rachel: "Give me children or I am dead." Esau: "I am about to die, so what need have I of birthrights" (25:32).

[22] Surely it is significant that the essence of idolatry is the confusion of object for subject (of *having* for *being),* while the essence of the monotheistic definition as pronounced by God in the Exodus narrative (Ex. 3:14) is "I am that I am."

is earned and deserved as an independent being. If one's early identity is grounded in love that is possessive, there may consequently follow an illusion of the mode of possessing as a substitute for—or conduit toward—a grounded sense of being. The birthright, like the blessings later on, can be artificially obtained by *being* Esau, but they cannot really become Jacob's until he struggles head-on, face to face, with his own sense of self. That is to say, he can only truly be blessed if Jacob can become Jacob.

By choosing implicit moral judgment, discernible only through the use of the "wrong" or anomalous word—וַיָּזֶד, the narrative voice has mirrored Jacob's own resistance to self-judgment.[23] But through the continuation of the story, we shall demonstrate (through further attention to strange word choice and other indicators of Jacob's repressed moral autonomy),[24] that Jacob is no less morally perturbed by his own behavior than is the reader. For Jacob, however, the emergence of the repressed subconscious and the confrontation with self will remain a struggle to be conducted at a dust-filled river-crossing in the distant future.

A final irony, that may further underscore the implicit moral critique on the part of the narrative voice, appears in the verse that follows the lentil stew for birthright barter. Immediately following the exploitation by Jacob of the **famished** Esau, the first verse of the following chapter (Gen. 26) reads: "And there was **famine** in the land. . . ."

---

[23] Though clearly the word "*vayazed*" here means "to cook," and is consistent with the word for a stew—"*nazid*," the fact that the words *vayazed* appears only here in the Bible with this meaning—and the term *nazid* appears in only two other contexts in the entire Bible—makes clear that the text implies a connective to the more common use of the word as denoting malice or moral culpability.

[24] I am aware that I have, to some extent, inverted the classic Freudian formulation of "repression" in these remarks. Freud thought of the most basic part of one's self as the id, a repository of emotions and desires that are often repressed by an external (and ultimately internalized) voice of societal or parental authority. It is this moral voice that represses the more basic level of self as emotion or desire. In my reading of the biblical text, it is Jacob's moral instincts that are essential to his being himself and to his being whole, and this moral autonomy is artificially repressed because of his desires and emotional needs.

CHAPTER THREE

"I AM ESAU":
INTEGRITY AND DIS-INTEGRATION OF
SELF

"When Isaac was old, and his eyes became dim, he called to Esau his older son and said to him, 'my son' (בני) and he said to him, 'Here am I' (הנני)." (Gen. 27:1)

Readers cannot help but hear the echo of the dialogue of father and son (Abraham and Isaac) at Mt. Moriah. In both scenes the vulnerable Isaac utters a trembling one word initiation of contact, at Moriah—"**avi**" (my father) and here—"**b'ni**" (my son). In both scenes, the response is also one powerful word, "הנני" ("Here am I"). Both scenes involve the conferral of divine blessing and both contain the possibility of Isaac's impending death. Is it surprising then, that Isaac orders the killing of an animal "in order that **my soul bless thee** before I die"?[1]

---

[1] The appearance of the word *nefesh* or soul as the subject of the verb *to bless*—תברכך נפשי is highly unusual in the Hebrew Bible, only appearing three additional times in this story (verses 19, 25, and 31) and a total of five times in Psalms 103

Rebecca has been eavesdropping and when Esau leaves to hunt venison, she turns to Jacob saying, "your father has spoken to Esau your brother saying bring me hunt and prepare a dish for me, and I will eat and **I will bless you before God** before I die."

Now Rebecca has indeed paraphrased Isaac's words and has conveyed the gist of his intention. Yet, a close reading will reveal that she has changed something significant, and therein might be the key to the tragic misunderstanding between husband and wife. Whereas Isaac spoke of the *blessing of his soul,* Rebecca has taken this to mean *a blessing before God.* Rebecca understands that Isaac is about to deliver the prophetic promise, the fulfillment of which she has anticipated ever since the struggle of her twins in the womb. Nachmanides points out as well that the term *"before God"* only appears in this entire episode in the words of the prophecy-driven Rebecca. Moreover, in Isaac's various blessings, the term never appears and despite some references to God, the closest we get to the covenantal language of blessing is given not to Jacob as Esau, nor in the second blessing to Esau, but in the third blessing given to Jacob as Jacob.[2] Only then does Isaac bestow the "blessing of Abraham," and only there does the blessing

---

and 104. It has been translated here in Genesis 27 variously as "my own blessing," "my special blessing," "my innermost blessing," all possible translations because the word *nefesh* often means *self.* In conversation, Professor Moshe Greenberg has suggested that of the range of possible meanings for *nefesh*, from the most concrete sense of *airway* or *gullet* or *opening of the throat* (see Isaiah 5:14 and Jonah 2:6), to the most abstract or subtle *soul*, the leading candidate here should be *the gullet*, in light of the context—"bring it to me and I will **eat** it, in order that my *nefesh* bless thee." According to Greenberg, the old, frail, Isaac is calling for food to refresh and invigorate him in order to have the strength to bless properly. This interpretation is certainly preferable to *my very own blessing,* because it does not take the Hebrew's "subject-verb" syntax and convert it to a "noun-adjective" construct. Either way, however, in light of the previous parallel verse that describes Isaac's love for Esau as conditional or situational, depending on food (Gen. 25:28), one would be correct in seeing this phrase (in 27:4) as intimating that the blessing of Esau, like the love of Esau, is in need of artificial stimulus in order to be aroused in Isaac's soul.

[2] Gen. 28:3–4.

include the phrase, "to you and your descendants." From all of the above evidence then, it would be reasonable to conclude that the blessing Isaac had intended to give Esau was not the covenantal *"blessing of Abraham."* The blessing *"before God"* that Rebecca mistakenly feared was about to be given to the wrong son was, in fact, reserved by the blind Isaac throughout the charade for the absent Jacob!

If we are to understand that both Isaac *and* Rebecca intended the covenantal blessing to go to Jacob, then we have the makings of tragic misunderstanding indeed. Moreover, we have yet another instance of the pattern of irony wherein Jacob employs circuitous (duplicitous?) means to receive that which he would have received in any case. The core of this drama, then, is not that of a blind man's confusion—of Isaac failing to know Jacob, nor is it the drama of ambiguity as to whom God's chosen will be. It is, rather, the comedy of miscommunication between Isaac and Rebecca and the internal drama of Jacob failing to know himself. It is ultimately the story of an alienation from self or *dis-integration* of identity so profound as to have Jacob believe he can receive the blessings only as Esau.

As we have discussed, the unloved (by father) Jacob, who has already gone to lengths to obtain the birthright, is in great psychological need of Isaac's blessing. It is Rebecca, however, who orchestrates the deception by which the blind Isaac will bless Jacob instead of Esau:

> "Now my son, listen to my voice, to that which I command you. Go please to the flocks and fetch me from there two good she goats so that I may prepare them as a dish for your father in the manner that he loves. And bring it to your father and he will eat, so that he will bless you before he dies." (Gen. 27:8–10)

What is Jacob's reaction to his mother's scheme to deceive Isaac and to receive the blessing? Are there traces of moral equivocation or principled resistance?

To those exegetes who claim that there need be no moral issue here because Jacob had already purchased the birthright, our answer would be multiple. To begin with, if this were Jacob's moral position, should he not have responded to his mother, saying "There is no need for subterfuge, Mother; I have purchased the right to the blessing fair and square." And if he cannot respond this way or cannot divulge to Isaac the particulars of the lentil soup scene, is it not because he is aware of the dubious morality of the barter? Indeed, if the barter of broth for birthright entitles him legally, but is so "heel-sneak"-like that he cannot openly claim his legal right, is this not yet another example of the pattern described above?

Secondly, it is clear that the biblical record treats *birthright* and *blessing* as separate entities, despite their obvious connection and the similarity of the Hebrew terms *beracha* (blessing) and *bechora* (birthright). Certainly, Esau regards them as two separate entities as he cries out to his father, "Is he not thusly called Jacob [usurper] for he has usurped [literally: "Jacob"ed me] **twice**; first he took away my birthright and now he has taken away my blessing!"

Furthermore, the literary evidence of Jacob's culpability in the deception scene is found throughout Genesis and elsewhere in the Bible. As Nehama Leibowitz and others have shown, the entire second half of Genesis may be said to consist of poetic justice (the Hebrew term is מדה כנגד מדה—measure for measure) for the deception.[3] Jacob is forced to flee from his parental home. He is deceived by Laban (his mother's brother), who disguises the older Leah as the younger Rachel who had been promised to Jacob. When Laban justifies his treachery, he says to Jacob, "It is simply not done in **our** place, to give the younger before the firstborn" (Gen. 29:26). Though previously Rachel and Leah had been referred to as the "big one and the little one," here Laban changes word choice, underscoring the **bekhira** (firstborn) and the **tze'ira** (younger),

---

[3] See the essay of Nehama Leibowitz, *"Your Brother Came With Deceit"* in *Studies in Bereishit* (Jerusalem: WZO, 1973) 264–270.

just in case Jacob or the reader failed to take proper note of the irony.

Later, Jacob's sons want to kill their brother Joseph—resulting in the disintegration of that family unit, just as Esau's oath to kill Jacob as a result of the deception splits the earlier family unit. Moreover, the brothers deceive Jacob by dipping Joseph's ornamented tunic[4] in the blood of a *goat* se'ir izim שעיר עזים. This mechanism of deception sends us back to the deception scene, where Jacob is concerned that the ruse will not work because Esau is *hairy* (Hebrew: se'ir שעיר, the same word for *goat*) and his mother responds by dressing him with the skins of the same *goats, izim*—עזים, that are to masquerade as venison.

I have not seen other commentaries remark on the connection between Leviticus 19:11, 14 and our story, though the phenomenon of legal sections of the Bible recapitulating various narratives is well evidenced in general, and with regard to the Jacob story in particular.[5] In those verses we read, "You shall not steal; you shall not deal deceitfully or falsely with your fellow. . . you shall not. . . place a stumbling block before the *blind*." Shall we not see here the resolution in legal terms of that which remained implicit, though heavily indicated, in the narrative section?

In later books of the Bible it becomes clear that Jacob has occasionally become a code-word or paradigm for brotherly treachery, most notably in Jeremiah 9:3 where we read:

"...וְעַל-כָּל-אָח אַל-תִּבְטְחוּ, כִּי כָל-אָח עָקוֹב יַעְקֹב..."

"...trust not [even] your brother, for every brother will *take advantage and usurp* [Hebrew: every brother will *akob Jacob*]."[6]

---

[4] I've used the more precise translation of the NJPS, rather than the more commonly used "coat of many colors."

[5] See, for example, Deut. 21:15–17: "If a man have two wives, one loved and the other despised, and both have borne him children, but the son of the despised is the first born, he may not treat as first-born the son of the loved one. . . ." Clearly there is legal encapsulation here to what is left as only the *implied* message of the Jacob-Leah-Rachel-Joseph imbroglio.

[6] See also Hosea 12:1–4.

Again, the text chooses not to utter the neat and tidy moral message that might have sounded something like the refrain of the Book of Judges—"and they did evil in the eyes of the Lord." Instead it risks the reading that we do indeed find in apologetic approaches like that of Rashi, who manages to maintain a positive moral judgment of Jacob even in light of Isaac's own pronouncement to Esau, "Your brother has come in treachery."[7] Perhaps the text prefers the implicit moral posture of disapproval because of the far more sophisticated (and more artistically satisfying) technique of expressing judgment through indirect parallel and intertextual reference. Additionally, the narrative voice may have refrained from explicit condemnation of Jacob in order to mirror Jacob's own resistance to his guilt. This resistance—a defensive measure of cognitive dissonance that allows Jacob to proceed without confronting his own moral debacle—becomes a crucial part of the evolving drama. And this brings us back to the question of Jacob's reaction to his mother's scheme. Even if we are convinced that the biblical narrative in its larger context sees the deception as shameful treachery, we must search the text for signs of Jacob's own moral instincts or repressions.

At first glance, there is no indication at all of a troubled conscience. Rebecca, for her part, may have dealt with any natural qualms by relying on the (mistaken) notion that the prophetic promise of blessing was in danger of being subverted. Moreover, she may have acted upon the further mistaken notion that any means would be justified in rectifying a potential derailing of the divine plan that had been revealed to her during pregnancy. Jacob's response, however, consists of the following objection:

---

[7] See his comment on Genesis 27:19, and his rendering of 27:35, "your brother came in treachery" as "came in cleverness," all based on Midrashic sources. Note nonetheless that other Midrashic sources read the story as we have, such as *Tanchuma Yashan*, *Vayetze* 11 (quoted in Leibowitz).

"But my brother Esau is a hairy man and I am smooth, perhaps my father will feel me and I shall be a trickster in his eyes, and I will bring upon myself a curse and not a blessing." (27:11–12)

On the surface, there is only one hesitation on the part of Jacob—the scheme has a practical flaw and might not succeed. The flaw might bring about the opposite of the desired result. On Piaget's or Kohlberg's scale of moral development, Jacob's moral intuition would be seen as unevolved at best. The sole impediment to crime—he might get caught before the blessing is procured.[8] In fact, it seems that what allays his fears and allows him to proceed is the dubious promise of Rebecca that even if the result proves disastrous, "the curse [which you fear] will fall upon me, my son" (27:13).

We must pause for a moment and absorb the full import of this exchange between mother and son. If Jacob is capable of detaching his own moral sense—as well as his culpability—from his behavior, is this not the very essence of alienation from self? Would an integrated identity be capable of relinquishing autonomy to the point of completely following the instructions of a mother in deceiving a father and believing that somehow the responsibility for one's own actions can be assumed by another? The scene begins with Jacob subsuming his own identity into that of his mother and concludes with his assuming the identity of his brother. For him, it is as if Rebecca has dressed up as Esau. No wonder this simple dweller of tents is capable of responding, "I am Esau your first born" (27:19). He is,

---

[8] I stress here the fear of being caught *before* the blessing is given because, as some commentaries have noted, the plan of Rebecca and Jacob could not have included the illusion that the deception would never be discovered, as eventually Esau would return from the field with venison. The plan must therefore have been to get the blessing before the return and to thereby obtain an irrevocable blessing, even at the cost of a rupture with Isaac and Esau and of the permanent stain of deception attending the blessing. The notion that the divine blessing can and should be obtained—regardless of moral consequence or collateral damage to brother and father —is perhaps the crux of the story's message and will be examined later.

in his mind, a marionette uttering the words of a ventriloquist, as he is operating in complete dissociation from self.

As we have said earlier, we can explain, though not justify, his disassociation, as the text has laid the psychological groundwork for his situation. He is the son of parents with differential love. His mother has compensated for the absence of Isaac's ability to show love and has created a relationship of dependence. At a pivotal moment she exercises the force of that dependence in order to procure for her son the very object of his desperate need.

Yet, even if we are led by the text to see Jacob as completely resistant to his identity as an autonomous moral being about to commit an immoral act, we shall be looking for those ripples in the surface reality that point to the repressed level of the unconscious. We are aware that as in Freud's metaphor, one can push the experience of moral or existential discomfort into the cellar and we can lock the door. But there will be a persistent knock on the cellar door discernible to those who recognize the language of the subconscious.

One such ripple in the surface of the text was noticed by the 19th century commentary **Haktav Ve'Hakabbala** (Rabbi Yaakov Zvi Mecklenberg) in his comments on "אולי ימושני אבי"—"*Perhaps my father will feel me*" (27:12):[9]

> **"Perhaps my father will feel me:** The word "פן—*lest*" implies that the speaker does not wish the matter to come to pass—it has a negative undertone, cf.: '*lest* he put forth his hand and take too of the tree of life' (Gen. 3:22) or '*lest* we be scattered about on the face of the earth' (Gen. 11:4).... Had Jacob wished to express the hope that his father **not** feel him, he should have said "*lest*—פן my father feel me." From here it would seem that Jacob did not favor the attempt to deceive his father and that he preferred to let the matter proceed without intervention.... Jacob hoped that

---

[9] Quoted and translated in Leibowitz, *Studies*, 264–5.

his mother would cancel the attempt as a result of his plea. Thus, he said, "perhaps"—"אולי". The word *perhaps* (אולי) is used when the speaker *desires* the matter to come to pass."

As Leibowitz (using this distinction of Mecklenberg) has concluded, "Jacob's inner reluctance and distaste for the strategy is thus revealed in the choice of adverbial prefix to his reply to his mother's importunings."[10] To infer from this fine distinction between פן and אולי (*lest* and *perhaps*) a conscious choice of words on the part of Jacob (as is the thrust of the comment of the pre-Freudian work—*Haktav Ve'hakabbala*) is not as convincing as seeing it as parapraxis or Freudian slip.[11] Jacob's use of the inappropriate word betrays an unconscious discomfort that is revealed in such a hidden way to the reader precisely because it remains hidden to Jacob himself. For Jacob, it is a slip of tongue that goes unnoticed by Rebecca, and by himself. For the biblical narrative, it is an intentionally artful "slip of pen," gratefully noted by the reader.

As we continue to study the stories of Jacob leading up to the struggle at Jabok, we will take note of numerous other instances of parapraxis on the part of Jacob. Most instances of parapraxis will point back to the repressed moral conflict that attends Jacob's role in the deception scene and to the sense of lack of entitlement that is both a cause and a result of his behavior there. One such instance will occur on the eve of the greatly feared reunion with Esau after decades of separation. The last time they were together, Esau vowed to kill him and now the circumstances threaten to make good the earlier desire, as Esau advances toward him with four

---

[10] Ibid, p. 265.

[11] The distinction is borne out by the consistent usage of *lest* vs. *perhaps* throughout the Bible with at least two other exceptions that prove the point. Both in Gen. 24:5 (as noted by the Midrash in *Bereishit Rabbah*) and in Job 1:5, the term *perhaps* is used instead of the appropriate *lest*. In both of these cases too, however, it would be well argued that the "wrong choice" of word is again attributable to unconscious motivation or inner conflict.

hundred men, a veritable army. Jacob hastily attempts to preempt enmity with a peace offering of enormous proportions. The two hundred she-goats (*Izim*—remember them from the deception scene?) are mentioned first, followed by hundreds of other livestock, all described both by the narration and by Jacob's own dialogue (five times) as an offering **מנחה** (*mincha*). But when Jacob finally meets Esau face to face, he uses the term *mincha* interchangeably with the word *berakha* (blessing). "And Jacob said, 'If I have please found favor in your eyes, take my offering from my hands. . . please take my *blessing* that is brought to you. . .'" (Gen. 33:10–11). He means to say *mincha* but the word comes out *berakha*. This issue of the blessing is the real score that must be settled, and it is not just between him and Esau, but also between Jacob and his unconscious, between Jacob and his guilt.

In that same scene, when expressing his fear of death at the hands of his brother, Jacob turns to God in prayer, and in doing so uses a very unusual and telling turn of phrase. "Please save me from the hand of my brother, **the hand of Esau**, for I am afraid of him lest [here he does use *lest*] he come and smite me **אם על בנים**—*mother in addition to child*." (Gen. 32:12). Literally, the phrase *mother in addition to child* reads *mother over* or **on top of** *children*. (Much in the same way, in English we may say *on top of* as a synonymous phrase for *in addition to*.) In only two other verses is an identical or nearly identical phrase ((**אם על בנים** used in the Hebrew Bible.[12] One appearance of the phrase is in the command of Deuteronomy 22:6–7 to send away the mother bird before taking its chicks or eggs. The command contains the phrase, "do not take the *mother and child*—**אם על הבנים**, again, literally, "the mother over the children"—the latter secondary meaning (by way of wordplay) supported by the use of the Hebrew word

---

[12] The third appearance of the phrase is in the later minor prophet Hosea, Chapter 10, verse 14. See also the *Midrash Bereishit Raba* 76:6. I should note, however, that using the word על to mean *in addition to* does appear in verses elsewhere, such as in Judges 15:8, where the verb is also *to smite*.

על (*upon*) thrice before in the verse with the meaning "upon" or "over" in conveying the image of a mother bird hovering protectively over the nest of her young.[13]

It would seem that Jacob has used an odd and nearly unique phrase to describe his fear of Esau's retribution when he speaks of the smiting of "*mother on top of sons.*" He has unwittingly betrayed a subconscious association of his present predicament with the hovering mother Rebecca of the deception scene and with his having relinquished his moral autonomy out of filial loyalty to her managerial dictates.[14]

Returning to 32:12 that ends with *mother on top of sons,* the verse begins with another unusual phrase that only appears here and in the masquerade scene. When Jacob appeals to God to save him from **"the hand of Esau"** are we not to refer back to the only other reference to "the hands of Esau" in the entire Bible? Is Jacob again betraying his unconscious fixation with the deception scene where his father momentarily suspects Jacob's trickery and masquerade and says to him," the voice is the voice of Jacob, but the **hands are the hands of Esau"**? As we shall see, the "*hands of Esau*" turn out to be the decisive factor in deceiving the suspicious Isaac.

The reason for the timing of these instances of parapraxis as "knocks on

---

[13] "כי יקרא קן צפור לפניך בדרך בכל עץ או **על** עץ או **על** הארץ... והאם רבצת **על** האפרוחים או **על** הביצים לא תקח האם **על** הבנים" (Deut. 22:6).

[14] The Talmud indeed suggests that the commandment "not to take the mother bird together with the sons" is connected to the biblical ideal of respecting the unique relationship of parent and child. In Tractate *Kiddushin* 39b (Babylonian Talmud), it is suggested that this thematic connection accounts for the fact that in the Bible only these two specific commandments (i.e., honoring father and mother and sending away the mother bird) are accompanied by a promised reward of long life. I find it curious that the two verses are linked not only by their containing the extremely rare use of the phrase *mother over sons,* but also indirectly through the immediately previous verse in Deuteronomy that speaks of the prohibition of masquerade. Might we understand the prohibition of "a man shall not don the garments of a woman" (Deut. 22:5) as an oblique intertextual reference to Rebecca dressing Jacob for the purpose of masquerade?

the cellar door of the unconscious" is obvious. The dissonance of Jacob's repressed memory and moral conflict grows louder and louder in chapter thirty-two with the anticipation and dread which accompany the coming reunion with Esau.

Returning to chapter 27, our scene reaches its moment of "truth" with the falsehood and irony of the following exchange: (Note the excessive repetition of "my son," "my father," "his son," and "his father." This repeated secondary identification is particularly noteworthy in a text known for its economy of language. Where words deliver no additional information [denotation], they must be read as loaded with evocative weight [connotation].)

18) And he came to **his father** and said, "**my father**" and he said, "Here am I, who are you **my son**"?

19) And Jacob said to **his father**, "I am Esau your firstborn; I have done as you have spoken to me, rise now and sit and eat from my venison in order that your soul will bless me."

20) And Isaac said to **his son**, "What is it that you have so quickly found **my son**?" And he said, "The Lord your God has given me good fortune."

21) And Isaac said to Jacob," Come hither and I will feel you **my son**, are you indeed Esau **my son** or are you not?"

22) And Jacob approached Isaac **his father** and he felt him, and he said, "the voice is the voice of Jacob, but the hands are the hands of Esau."

23) And he did not recognize him, for his hands were as the hairy hands of Esau **his brother**, and he blessed him.

[The text supplies us with a false ending to the deception as both Jacob and the reader breathe a sigh of relief with the concluding words of verse twenty-three, "and he blessed him." The unbearable tension has broken and subsided. And then like the final lunge of the predator (who was assumed to have been neutralized) at the feet of the prematurely relieved prey, Isaac asks one last time]:

24) And he said, "Is it really you Esau, **my son**"? And he said, "It is I."

And only here does the denouement begin with the concluding verses:

25) And he said, "Bring it to me and I shall eat from the hunt of **my son**, so that my soul will bless you"; and he served him wine and he drank.
26) And Isaac **his father** said to him, "Come hither and kiss me, **my son**."
27) And he approached and kissed him, and he [Isaac] smelled the fragrance of his clothing and he blessed him and said, "the fragrance of **my son** is like the fragrance of the field that God has blessed."

One is struck by the blind Isaac's poignant use of all other senses in ascertaining the identity of his son. Sound, smell, taste, and touch are all involved as Isaac unwittingly forces Jacob deeper and deeper into deception. As taste and smell are called upon by Isaac in his efforts to bring forth blessing from his soul, readers will recall the relationship between imminent death, blessings and the smell of burnt meat—both here and at the binding of Isaac at Moriah. It would seem that Isaac, in calling upon taste and smell, is aware (at least subliminally) of the phenomenon of which Proust spoke in the well-known passage in which taste and smell, even after "things are broken and scattered," and even after the people are gone, remain poised to reconstruct memory.[15]

How ironic must the concluding words of the following verse containing *Jacob as Esau*'s blessing have sounded to the ears of Jacob *his son:*

> 28) "... be a master to your brother and the sons of your mother will bow down to you, your cursers will be cursed and those who bless you shall be blessed."

Jacob's mother's earlier assurance, that if a curse will result from his subterfuge "the curse will fall upon me, my son" (Gen. 27:13), represented an impossible and ironic instance of parental denial of the child's moral autonomy and accountability. Was Jacob aware—at least on some level of the unconscious—of this impossibility? Moments later, Isaac assures Jacob that the "sons of your mother"—the very object of Jacob's impersonation—will bow down, and that curses and blessings will find their rightful destination. Is the irony addressed only to the reader? Does the literary ploy imply the register of irony upon Jacob's unconscious as well?

How many times must Jacob's unconscious have played over the repeated question of Isaac? "Who are you, my son? Yes, but really, who are you?" How many times must Jacob have returned to the numerous points

---

[15] "And so it is with our own past. It is a labour in vain to attempt to recapture it: all the efforts of our intellect must prove futile. The past is hidden somewhere outside the realm, beyond the reach of intellect, in some material object (in the sensation which that material object will give us) of which we have no inkling. . . . perhaps because of those memories, so long abandoned and put out of mind. . . the shapes of things. . . were either obliterated or had been so long dormant as to have lost the power of expansion which would have allowed them to resume their place in my consciousness. But when from a long distant past nothing subsists, after the people are dead, after the things are broken and scattered, **taste and smell alone**, more fragile but more enduring, more unsubstantial, more persistent, more faithful, remain poised along time, **like souls**, remembering, waiting, hoping, amid the ruins of all the rest; and bear unflinchingly, in the tiny and almost impalpable drop of their essence, the vast structure of recollection." Marcel Proust, *Swann's Way* (NY: Random House, 1989) 47–51.

at which he could have retreated, to the opportunities Isaac gave him for withdrawal? How many times over the ensuing decades of exile from his parents did he hear the echo of his own twice repeated response, "I am Esau, your firstborn. . . . It is I"? Are we to assume that the rhythmic insistence of the terms *his father, my son* (*your brother*—at the end) that so sting the reader, fall on the seemingly deaf ears of Jacob without lasting impression?

And yet, Jacob is decidedly not portrayed as a *Raskolnikov*, perpetually and unbearably plagued by conscience. In fact, when confronted by the weighty evidence of poetic justice later in life, Jacob is more offended than chastened, more bewildered than introspective. It seems that the *dis-integration* of self is so extensive, the dissociation necessary to produce the convincing performance of "I am Esau" so profound, and the cognitive dissonance with regard to his mother's and his own moral behavior so compelling, as to have thrust all internal conflict into the realm of the unconscious. We will again look to parapraxis as well as to Jacob's dream in the following scene for evidence of the internal struggle for integration. For such a man as Jacob cannot live life indefinitely without integrating earthly behavior with a higher morality. Even if only in dreams, the language of the unconscious, there must be a connecting ladder or ramp between heaven and earth, a way to integrate his disconnected worlds.

CHAPTER FOUR

OF DREAMS AND VOWS

After Esau enters and Isaac discovers the deception, Isaac tells Esau that, in effect, the die has been cast. Words uttered have created a reality that cannot be reversed. "I have already made him master to you, and all his brothers have I given to him as servants. . . and what can I still do for you, **my son**?" Esau responds that there must be more than one possible blessing, and he cries.

In response, Isaac gives him the following "mixed" blessing:

> ". . . and behold your abode will be of the fat of the land, and of the dew of the heavens above. And you will live by your sword and will serve **your brother**. And when you shall achieve dominance, you will break his yoke from off your neck."

In an artistically ambiguous statement, the next verse reads, "and Esau hated Jacob for the blessing that his father blessed *him*." Who is the antecedent of "him"; does it refer to Jacob's blessing or to his own? In other words, does Esau hate on account of the blessing Jacob took, or because of the dubious blessing that was left for him? The ambiguity leads us to either interpretation, and therefore to both.[1] The result of the hatred is, however, unambiguous:

> "... And Esau said, 'soon the days of **my father's** mourning will approach and I will kill Jacob, **my brother**.' And Rebecca was told of the words of Esau **her older son** and she called for Jacob **her younger son** and said to him, 'Behold, Esau **your brother** is consoling himself with plans to kill you. Now listen to my voice, **my son**, and flee at once to **my brother** Laban in Haran.'"

Again, as in the scene of the deception, the almost rhythmic repetition of the family relationships ironically highlights the betrayal and rupture of those relationships. And yet again, Rebecca is orchestrating. However, here there is no motherly assurance (nor can there be) of the likes of "עלי קללתך בני—your curse will fall upon me, my son" (Gen. 27:13). The continuation of that original verse reads: *"and just listen to my voice and go [retrieve two tasty goats for the deception]."* (This was a repetition of the exhortation of Rebecca six verses earlier when she said, *"And now my son, listen to my voice."*) At this juncture, after the deception has led to the murderous hatred of Esau, Rebecca uses the very same words, *"and now my son listen to my voice...and rise up and flee...."* By putting the very same phrase yet again in the mouth of Rebecca, the text underscores the irony of her previous assurances that Jacob will not suffer harm from their deception. Now she tells Jacob with the same voice of authority that *he* must pay the price of threatened fratricide and exile. It seems there are objective limitations even to a mutually agreed upon pact of "אם על בנים—*mother over sons,*" and there is an unavoidable price to be paid (in practical and in psychological terms) for the surrender of one's moral autonomy.[2]

---

[1] See Hizkuni (13th century exegete) to Gen. 27:41.
[2] The most apt Talmudic principle expressing the idea that one cannot avoid culpability on the claim that one is acting at the bidding of another is the phrase,

Jacob flees to Haran, to the home of his mother's brother, Laban. Irony, again, abounds. Rebecca and Jacob have deceived Isaac in order to procure "the blessing of Abraham" (a blessing he would have received in any case, as pointed out earlier). The original blessing to Abraham is delivered in Haran and is contingent upon Abraham leaving Haran and journeying to Canaan.[3] Now, as a result of subterfuge, Jacob who was to advance toward the divine destiny of Abraham, regresses, reversing destination and heading from Canaan back to Haran. The reversal of geographic destination signals reversal of prophetic destiny.[4] This is, I believe, one of the central messages of the book of Genesis. Sacrifice of moral autonomous choice, and resorting to dubious means to achieve even the most lofty or divinely mandated visions, constitutes a violation of the very divine will it is intended to serve.

The irony also proceeds on the more mundane territory of storyline. The possessor of newly acquired blessings that include family leadership and wealth of grain and wine, is now homeless and alone, and as his own words will indicate, unsure of the most basic provisions of bread or clothing. On the way, he makes an unanticipated stop,[5] is overcome with sleep, and dreams an unanticipated dream:

"And he dreamed and *behold* a ladder[6] set on the ground, its top

---

אין שליח לדבר עבירה—"there is no proxy in matters of sin," see Babylonian Talmud, Tractate *Kiddushin* 42a. Here, to make matters worse, the passage further underscores the irony by having Rebecca tell Jacob to stay away long enough for Esau to forget "what *you* have done to him" (Gen. 27:45). When things go sour, where is mutual responsibility, let alone the notion of proxy?

[3] See Gen. 11:31, and 12:1. Abraham was in Haran when he received the divine call to leave his father's house.

[4] I am grateful to Mr. Daniel Shapiro, my nephew, for pointing this out to me.

[5] The Hebrew words used in this verse (Gen. 29:11) are ויפגע במקום, literally: "he bumped into the place."

[6] I have used the common translation, *ladder,* though the term סלם is unique in the Hebrew Bible, and might be more accurately defined as *ramp.* See Harold Cohen, *Hapax Legomena in the Light of Akkadian and Ugaritic* (Missoula, Montana:

reaching to the sky, and angels of God ascending and descending upon it. And behold the Lord was standing above it [alternatively —above *him],* and He said,' I am the Lord the God of *your father Abraham and the God of Isaac.....*"

Even before examining the content of the dream or of God's message in the dream, we may have already encountered one of its most telling elements, again through the use of "the wrong" choice of words. More than a millennium before Freud, the Talmud records the observation of a Rabbi Samuel son of Nachmani who said in the name of Rabbi Jochanan that in dreams, "a person is shown nothing if not the inner thoughts of his own heart" (BT, Tractate *Berakhot* 55b). Notwithstanding the 12th century exegete Abraham Ibn Ezra's distinction between regular dreams and dreams of prophecy,[7] we are struck by the appositional phrase *"your father"* attached to the grandfather Abraham and not to Isaac. It seems clear that in Jacob's "inner thoughts of heart" the Lord who will comfort him will be the Lord of Abraham *his father.* As for the God of Isaac (his genetic father), there is a missing relational adjective, as the very situation that begs comfort, Jacob's precarious homeless state, is a result of his having betrayed the father-son relationship. Here, the slip of tongue

---

Scholars Press, Society of Biblical Literature, 1978) 34.

[7] See Ibn Ezra to Genesis 28:11 and his argument with R. Samuel Hofni Gaon. I would certainly take issue with Meir Sternberg who admits that "the modern view of the dream as the expression of internal states and stresses has its precedents in antiquity," but claims that "this conception is foreign to the spirit of Biblical narrative," M. Sternberg, *The Poetics of Biblical Narrative* (Indiana Univ. Press, 1987) 395. The 10th century exegete Samuel Ben Hofni Gaon's comments on dream interpretation include the remark that in order to properly interpret a dream one must know the temperament of the dreamer and his particular circumstances. See *Peirush Hatorah L'Rav Shmuel ben Hofni Gaon* ed. A. Greenbaum (Jerusalem: Mosad Harav Kook, 1979) 112–114. Apparently, he made similar remarks on this passage concerning Jacob's dream of ascending angels, and these remarks are what occasioned Ibn Ezra's critique. Unfortunately, in the surviving manuscripts of Ben Hofni's commentary, this section is missing (see p. 114, note 56).

or anomalous wording appears in the words of the Lord as heard in the dream consciousness of Jacob.

The irony of this asymmetry (i.e., calling the grandfather "father" and then referring to Isaac without a relational identification) might alternatively be expressed by saying the following: The biblical text has God appearing to Jacob at this juncture as the God of *Abraham your father* but only as the *God of Isaac* [. . .], so as to subtly indicate to Jacob (and to the reader) the source of his predicament. Surely in a text so generous in its connotative use of relational appositives (i.e., the extensive and denotatively superfluous appearance of *my son, his father, your brother*, etc.), the absence of *his father* to describe Isaac and its "misplacement" upon Abraham cannot be incidental.

Returning to the words of God that accompany the vision of the ladder, Jacob is told that he and his seed will inherit the land, his seed will be as numerous as the dust of the earth, that he will burst forth west, east, north, and south, and that "all the families of the earth will be blessed through you." The last phrase is identical to the blessing given to Abraham in his first divine communication (Gen. 12:3). At this point in the dream, God turns to Jacob's more immediate and personal situation and declares: "Behold I am with you, and I will watch over you wherever you may go, and I will return you to this land, for I will not leave you [unaccompanied] until I have done all that I have spoken."

It would seem that in the dream, God has addressed all of the anxieties of the heart. The homeless Jacob is told that he will possess land, the lonely Jacob will have numerous offspring, the Jacob estranged from his family will not only have family but will be the source of blessing for *all families*. Most importantly, the great uncertainty of his tenuous status in the eyes of God after all that has happened is relieved by the assurance that God will be with him.

When Jacob awakens suddenly (ויִּיקַץ) from his dream, he is overcome with a sense of the presence of God, and utters the majestic words, "this is none other than the house of the Lord and the gateway to heaven." Yet, the very next words catch us by surprise. "And Jacob *arose early* וישכם in the morning. . ." Had Jacob fallen back asleep after such a remarkable revelation? Or are we to distinguish between ויקץ *to awaken* and וישכם *to arise early.* Whether he was lying awake the remainder of the night until he arose or had fallen back asleep, there will be a marked transition between the two awakenings. The sublime reflection of his initial awakening—a reflection stated in emphatic terms of certainty and knowledge: "Indeed! There is God in this place, and I had not known it!" (28:16)—subsequently descends in tone and substance to the tentative, conditional, and pragmatically grounded language of the morning—"if God will be with me. . . ."

If we are indeed to read the *awakening* as parallel yet distinct from his later *arising*, we may have here the record of two distinct stages in Jacob's internalization of the dream—two differential reflections of the residue of the unconscious or semi-conscious revelation. As will happen when one awakens suddenly in the night from a particularly vivid and portentous dream, one is struck with the power and novelty of the dream's insight. "Indeed!... I had not known it!" The dream, if receiving any verbal expression at that moment, is more likely at *that* point to bear the signature of the experience of epiphany. ("This is. . . the house of the Lord. . . the gateway to heaven.") But in the morning the same dream will have faded and what remains will have been translated into the context of one's reality, one's daytime consciousness. The lofty language of this epiphany will give way to the pragmatic attempt to integrate the dream into the categories of the here and now. This may account for some of the similarities and differences between the language of the subsequent vow and the dream that it parallels.[8]

---

[8] The subconscious processed at two levels has a parallel resonance when this dream of Jacob's is contrasted with his only other recorded dream, in Gen. 31:10–13. There, the vision of ascending (*olim*) and descending angels has made way for a vision of spotted and speckled sheep (going up—*olim*—upon each other). God then appears to him for the purpose of confirming his rights to a just financial reward for his

After arising early in the morning, before resuming his journey, Jacob is moved to utter a vow. The conditions of the vow (as opposed to the part of the vow that promises to perform certain acts if the conditions are fulfilled) will be transparently parallel to the promises of God in the dream of the night before, with several striking discrepancies:

Jacob's Vow	The Previous Night's Dream
(28:20) And Jacob pledged a vow, saying: if God will be with me	(28:15) Behold I will be with you
And will watch over me on this path upon which I go	And I will watch over you wherever you will go
And will provide me with bread to eat	—
And clothing to wear	—
(28:21) And I will return **in peace** to **my father's house**	And I will return you to **this land**
the Lord will be for me a God	I will not leave you

In the vow, Jacob has echoed only the divine promises that address his most immediate and personal needs (verse 15). In Jacob's vow there is no parallel to the long term promise to his seed in the previous night's dream (28:13–14). Also with regard to God's watching over him, Jacob takes

labor. When an angel does appear at the end of the dream, it is to tell him it is time to head back toward Beth-El, the site of his first dream, the site of the vow. In this context, as well as in the first dream, the verb פרץ—*to burst forth*—is used. In the first dream, Jacob and his seed will "*burst forth* ופרצת west and east and north and south and will be a blessing to all families of the earth." In this later episode (Gen. 30:43), Jacob "had *burst forth* ויפרץ greatly and now possessed many sheep." The similarity of language (פרץ) highlights the contrast between the initial dream of lofty covenantal promise and the pragmatic economic dream after two decades in Laban's house that conveys a new meaning to "counting sheep."

the more general and long range promise —*wherever you will go*—and converts it to present tense and immediate context—*this path upon which I go*. Jacob is too preoccupied with the present to contemplate the future. He is too mired in fate, to be able to focus on destiny. As we shall demonstrate, even this heroic figure will not be able to fashion the autonomous fulfillment of his divinely mandated destiny, while *bound by* and *to* the past by his own resistance to it. And as we shall see from the language of the vow itself, Jacob is subconsciously *bound* to the deception carried out with his mother in his "*father's house*" (the phrase introduced by Jacob in his pledge in verse 21).

God has promised Jacob that he will return *to the land*, but for Jacob the question involves the returning in *peace* שלום to *his father's house*. He is responsible for destroying that peace. He has disrupted the unity of his father's house, and now he turns to God to restore it. Most tellingly, Jacob adds two requests or conditions that do not parallel God's previous words, to "*give me bread to eat and clothing to wear,* ונתן לי לחם לאכל ובגד ללבש."

Where does this anxiety come from? Why does this particular language enter Jacob's vocabulary precisely at this point? Tellingly, Jacob's request does parallel another previous verse, unrelated to God's promise. A return to chapter 27, verse 15, will remind us that Rebecca "took the *clothing* of Esau her son . . . , and *dressed* [in Hebrew both *to wear* and *to dress* use the same verb root] Jacob her younger son." Both key Hebrew words appear— בגדי and ותלבש. In verse 17 there, Rebecca completes the preparations for deceiving Isaac as "she *gave* [ותתן—same verb root as ונתן] . . . the *bread* לחם she had made into the hands of Jacob, her son." Jacob asks of God to provide him with the basic needs for survival, but in doing so he has inserted into the request the very language of the betrayal scene! And he has revealingly highlighted this language by making the two requests the sole additions to a vow that otherwise parallels God's promises.

One might, in fact, point out that Jacob asks of God to provide him with that which was previously supplied by mother. A victim of his own relinquishing of autonomy to his mother who *gave him bread and dressed him with clothing*, he now turns to God and asks the same of Him! For what is the essence of a vow, if not the claim that at the present moment my autonomy (my control over my own fate) is severely limited. The logic of the vow then proceeds to say: *if* God will only take my fate into His hands, and provide me with that which under normal circumstances I would provide for myself, I promise to reciprocate when my autonomy is reinstated. The very essence of a vow is a recognition (or mistaken perception) of constricted autonomy.

What then shall we make of this parallel between the function of Rebecca and that of God for the constricted Jacob? One might infer that by surrendering his autonomy to Rebecca he has made a god of her, or that he has sinned against the autonomous and integrated self that God desires of us. Perhaps, more radically, we understand that he has responded to God out of the same (mistaken) sense of constricted autonomy that characterized his response to Rebecca. God is taken to be a nurturing, protective mother, as opposed to a sovereign who encourages, expects, and demands autonomy.

Strikingly, if one returns to the scene of the deception, there is a moment in which Isaac questions the masquerading Jacob as to how he was able to return so quickly from the hunt with a ready meal. Unable to reveal that Rebecca had provided the meal, Jacob prevaricates, saying: "because the Lord your God brought me good fortune."[9] Thus, the vow constitutes an echo of a previous "confusion" on the part of Jacob between God and Rebecca as the providers of sustenance. One might even suggest that this repeated confusion encapsulates the essential drama of these scenes. Should Jacob (or the reader) identify the machinations of Rebecca with the divine providence they are designed to advance? More generally, what is the appropriate relationship between the mandates of human behavior—such as

---

[9] Gen. 27:20.

moral autonomy and family loyalty—and the realization of a prophetically divine covenant?

As we return to the particulars of the vow, Jacob has pledged that if all of the conditions of verses 19 and 20 are fulfilled, the stone that he had placed as a monument shall become a house of God. Moreover, he will offer a tenth of all that God has given him in return.[10] The pledge will not be fulfilled for decades, as Jacob will overstay his refuge in Laban's house. Is it his fear of confronting Esau that will prevent Jacob from reasserting his autonomy and fulfilling the vow? Is it his fear of confronting himself that will keep him from Beth-El, and from returning to his father's house? In order to approach these questions, we must examine the dialectics of *vowing*, and the particular relationship of those dialectics to the personality of Jacob.

Unquestionably, there are truly moments and circumstances in life in which one's freedom or capacity to make choices and to advance one's destiny is limited. The Bible acknowledges this situation, and though it regards the making of vows as a regrettable default,[11] it provides the **temporarily** constricted person the option of substituting words for action. Words, always available (even to the prisoner in solitary confinement, let alone to the lonely traveler), can bridge the gap between intention and action by means of a sacred promise. God, in his benevolence, is called upon to consider the intended deed as if already performed, that is **temporarily**, until *word* can be matched with *action*. But herein lay the rub. Legitimate substitution of words (as pledge of intention) for action can occur only so long as there is indeed an "objective" constriction of autonomy. If the constriction is the product of pretense or illusion, the pledge amounts to an abuse of the concept of a sacred promise. In such a case, the vow does not

---

[10] I have chosen what I believe to be the most credible division of the vow into the two sections of condition vs. pledge—i.e., "if this. . . then that. . . ." However, the Hebrew syntax of the vow certainly allows for alternative readings. See Leibowitz, *Studies in Bereishit*, 305–309.

[11] See Ecclesiastes 5:4, "Better not to vow than to vow and not to pay."

assist in overcoming the *dis-integration* of self by uniting words as intention with eventual result and action. On the contrary, a vow that *unnecessarily* substitutes words for action actually hinders the process of integration by artificially perpetuating the gap between them. Thus, even a legitimate vow becomes "sinful" or counterproductive if the one who pledges fails to make good on the promise at the earliest possible opportunity.

For this reason, the prohibition in Deuteronomy 23:22 reads: "If you shall vow a vow to the Lord your God, you *shall not be late* לא תאחר in paying it. . . ." The use of the verb אחר (to be *late* or *behind*) here will be highly significant as we trace the repetition of this word in Jacob's vocabulary and his use of it to describe himself to Esau when they finally reunite. In 32:5, Jacob will send a message to Esau, saying: "I have sojourned with Laban and have been *late* ואחר until now [twenty-two years!]." Recall that the very literal meaning of the name *Jacob* is "to come from behind," to come out *late*, or second.

The ancient Midrash Tanchuma has commented both on the nature of unfulfilled vows and on the story of Jacob, in a striking, if cryptic, passage that reads as follows:

> "In several situations a person's ledger [his account book in heaven of merits and debits] is open: he who embarks on a journey at night and alone, he who sits in a house that tilts and shakes, and he who vows a vow and does not pay. . . as it says in Deuteronomy, 'if you vow a vow do not be late in paying'. . . Come and see, when Jacob went to Aram Naharayim what does Scripture say? 'and Jacob vowed a vow saying. . . etc. He became wealthy and settled in and did **not** pay his oath so God brought upon him Esau who sought to kill him. He [Esau] took from him all that gift of two hundred goats and still he did not sense it [the failure to pay the promised vow]. So God brought upon him the angel who wrestled with him in the mud nearly killing him. . . and he became lame. Since he did

not sense it, the trouble of Dinah [the rape of his daughter] came upon him. Because he [still] did not sense it, the trouble of Rachel [her premature death] came upon him. And the Holy One Blessed Be He said, 'until when will this righteous man be smitten and not sense for what sin he is smitten?' Behold I will inform him as it is said 'And the Lord spoke to Jacob, saying, 'Rise up and go to Beth-El' (Gen. 35:1). . . and make there an altar at the same place where you vowed to me. . . ."[12]

In interpreting this midrash, Avivah Zornberg has insightfully noted that the passage is not about exacting God's retribution for late payment of a debt, but is rather a comment on the dangerous "disequilibrium" created by an unfulfilled vow. Thus, the midrash equates dwelling in a teetering home and traveling at night without companionship to this precarious state of being.[13] Zornberg describes the "peculiar peril of the unfulfilled vow" in the following way:

"[T]o vow is to break a rational limitation, a clear boundary between hand and mouth. . . . If the mouth is not underwritten, as it were, by the hand, if words correspond to nothing, then one finds that one has created a reality—that is not—reality. . . . In making a vow, one constructs an image of an intended future, and thereby opens a Pandora's box of conflicts and resistances of hitherto hidden fears and fantasies: the ledger of one's inner being, in the imagery of the midrash, is exposed to searching angelic gaze. . . . The gap between hand and mouth is a perilous space. . . ."[14]

---

[12] Midrash *Tanchuma* (ed. Warsaw), *Vayishlach*, Section 8.
[13] It may be that the midrash chose these specific analogies because they are also descriptive of Jacob's situation. He is indeed traveling alone at night and has just escaped a household (his father's) on the verge of collapse.
[14] Avivah Gottlieb Zornberg, *Genesis: the Beginning of Desire* (Phila.: Jewish Publication Society, 1995) 222–3.

To carry the insight of the midrash further, to perpetuate the gap between word and action is to make of "loss of autonomy" a modality of being, instead of a temporary status as "a regrettable but unavoidable situation"; it is the equivalent of taking a dilapidated house and taking up permanent residence there. When Zornberg writes of the gap between hand and mouth, one is transported of necessity to the verse she might have quoted, "the voice is the voice of Jacob, but the hands are the hands of Esau." Esau (עשו) whose name means "action," is identified with *hands,* while Jacob, is represented by *voice,* by the medium of spoken (but unfulfilled) intention. Perhaps the text has placed in the mouth of the bewildered Isaac a foreshadowing of the synthesis necessary to create the covenantal family—a family whose destiny will neither suffer from the impulsivity of Esau's unreflective actions nor from the paralysis of a Jacob who forfeits autonomous action, and continually sees himself as bound by "*permanent circumstance.*" Perhaps Isaac has presciently reconciled the struggle of the two parts of the same covenantal womb in putting together the complementary "voice of Jacob" with the "hands of Esau."

In a sense, Jacob is not only late in the fulfillment of a vow, he *is* an unpaid vow! He lives in the gap between "hand and voice." This is not just true because he has created an artificial breach of identity between his Jacob's voice (the name of God is on his lips—see 27:20) and his "hands of Esau." It is true on another level, as well, because Jacob lives with an abiding self-perception of his own constricted autonomy. He has taken the idea of "vow" as situational and temporary limitation and has institutionalized it as a modus vivendi, a pattern for negotiating life.

Thus far, Jacob has deferred to Rebecca, and later to God, his sovereignty in determining his fate—avoiding the inner call to master his own destiny. This pattern will be repeated and escalated in his subsequent extended refuge in the house of his mother's brother.

CHAPTER FIVE

IN LABAN'S HOUSE

If one were to characterize Jacob's sojourn of refuge with his uncle and father-in-law Laban—the key description would be that of a life mortgaged to another. Jacob's lack of self-mastery is deftly if subtly underscored at every turn by the text's choice of language as well as by the storyline. Of course, to begin with, we have the deception of Jacob by Laban through masquerading the older as younger—giving him Leah for a wife instead of the promised Rachel. Here, the biblical pattern of divine *measure for measure* (poetic justice) is conveyed not simply by rewarding trickery with trickery, but in a deeper sense as well, as a character reaps the natural consequences of a process that he has set into motion. Through the act of relinquishing his moral autonomy and disassociating from his own identity (I am Esau), Jacob has become a man whose life is not his own. This carries into the most basic and intimate elements of identity, his family relations.

Laban decides, against Jacob's will, who it is that he will marry. Even the question of with whom he will cohabit on a given night is beyond Jacob's autonomy, as strikingly brought home by the episode of the mandrakes. "You will come unto me; for I have indeed **hired you** with my son's mandrakes." (Gen. 30:15). The *hiring* is entirely a result of negotiation between Leah and Rachel. Jacob is the object of their barter. When children are born, Leah and Rachel name them.[1] Though Eve named Cain and Seth, the common practice in the Bible is for the father to name the child, as is the case with Abraham naming Ishmael and Isaac, and Isaac naming Jacob.[2] Ever since the story of the Garden of Eden, naming is an expression of mastery, but it is beyond the limited dominion of Jacob.

In chapter thirty, verse twenty-five, Jacob finally decides to leave Laban after more than two decades of service and subservience. He asks permission to leave and to return to his own place, his own land. In verse 30:26 there is a remarkably telling choice of words by Jacob. He says to Laban, **"Give me my wives** and my children for whom I have served you. . . ." Twenty-some years have passed since Jacob said to Laban: (Gen. 29:21) **"Give me my wife. . . ."** Yet it seems that his wives are still not his own, and the paradox of needing someone else to *give you that which you call your own* is poignant. Apparently Laban understands all too well Jacob's sense of lack of entitlement and exploits it to the very end of their relationship as in their parting conversation he tells Jacob, "the daughters are *my* daughters, the sons are *my* sons, and the sheep are *my* sheep, and **all that you see** is *mine*. . ." (Gen. 31:43).

Here too, there is a poignant reversal, in which there is an ironic echo of the original language of the prophetic promise to Abraham in Genesis 13:15—"**all** [the land] **that you see** I will give to you. . . ." The language of possession has become the language of dispossession.[3] Even when Jacob

---

[1] The only children jointly named by Jacob and Rachel or Leah are Benjamin and Levi. The renaming by Jacob of Benjamin (born after leaving Laban's house) takes place after the tragic naming of Ben Oni (child of my suffering) by Rachel as she dies in childbirth.

[2] See Gen. 16:15, 21:3, 25:26. In the case of Esau, "they named him" (Gen. 25:25). It is not clear from the text to whom "they" refers. See Rashi.

[3] Here, there is yet another indication that "the blessing of Abraham"—dubiously attained at the end of the deception scenes (28:4)—has ironically reversed direction and receded from Jacob's grasp.

finally has his own family and is wealthy with flocks, he oddly still sees himself as disenfranchised. Psychically, they are not his wives, not his children, not his flocks.

In fact, the verses of Exodus 21:1–6—describing the servitude of the Hebrew slave—reflect this understanding that the wife and children given a servant by his master are not truly his own. "If his master gave him a wife and she has borne him children, the wife and her children shall belong to the master, and he shall leave alone."

David Silber has aptly pointed out that there are two other main differences between a laborer (in Hebrew: *oved*) and a slave (Hebrew: *eved*).[4] In these matters, as well, Jacob is more slave than laborer to Laban. A laborer should receive fair compensation and should be free to leave according to his will. The slave works disproportionately to his wages and leaves only with the permission of his master. In Chapter 31:20–24, when Jacob finally leaves after twenty two years of service to Laban in tending his sheep, he sneaks away like a thief. Indeed, Laban chases him and accuses him of "*stealing*" away. The biblical language used to describe Jacob's escape and the pursuit of Laban parallels precisely the language later used in Exodus to describe Pharaoh's view of the Israelite slaves' "escape" from Egypt and his subsequent pursuit:

> "**And it was told** to Laban that Jacob **had fled**. . . and **he chased after** him. . . ." (Gen. 31:22–23)

> "**And it was told** to the king of Egypt that the nation **had fled**. . . and **he chased after** the children of Israel." (Ex. 14:5–8)

> "**ויגד ללבן כי ברח** יעקב...**וירדף אחריו**"

---

[4] This was conveyed in Silber's lecture at Midreshet Lindenbaum in Jerusalem several years ago.

"וַיֻּגַּד לְמֶלֶךְ מִצְרַיִם כִּי בָרַח הָעָם...וַיִּרְדֹּף אַחֲרֵיהֶם"

Moreover, the other aspect that signifies a slave-like relationship with Laban—that of unfair wages—is reflected in the counter-claim that Jacob makes in response to his father-in-law's attack:

"You have switched my wages ten times over." (Gen. 31:41)

Further indication that Jacob's sense of lack of entitlement was tantamount to self-enslavement can be found in Jacob's response to Laban's earlier initiative. Laban, after enjoying his guest's free labor for a month, had appropriately made the following offer to Jacob:

"Because you are my brother should you work for me for nothing? Tell me *(hagida li)* what your wages shall be." (Gen. 29:16)

Jacob incredibly, almost preposterously, responds that he will work a full seven years in return for marrying Rachel, Laban's daughter. We can only imagine that Laban must have been all too happy to accept—though in concealing his glee, he responds with nonchalance, "better to give her to you than to another man." What could have *possessed* Jacob to have offered the outlandish seven years of free labor (and delayed gratification) in exchange for the right to marry Rachel? Love is one thing, incredibly poor negotiating skills another. Two intertextual references in this negotiation provide a broader context that may further clarify the conscious or unconscious motivation of the hapless Jacob.

First, the number of seven years of labor sends any student of the Bible back again to the famous verses in Exodus (21:1), where a divine commandment limits the number of years of servitude for the Hebrew slave to six years. ". . . And in the seventh year, he shall go forth free without cost." Only the stubborn slave who loves his servitude more than his freedom will sign on for further labor and as an indication of his foolish refusal to gain his freedom, his ear is pierced through at the doorway (Ex. 21:2–6).

More idiosyncratic a parallel is to be found in the narrative's description of Jacob's seven years of labor as but *"a few days* in his eyes..." (Gen. 29:20). The unusual Hebrew phrase for "a few days," כימים אחדים,[5] echoes the parting words of Rebecca to the fleeing Jacob, "And now my son, listen to me and arise and flee to Laban my brother... and dwell with him for **a few days** (ימים אחדים)... until your brother forgets what you have done to him, and I will send for you and take you back from there" (Gen. 27:43–44).

A man deeply in love with a woman might feel that every day of delay is like an eternity, but Jacob strangely experiences these seven years as "**the few days**" of which his mother spoke.

Jacob is willing to spend more time than is reasonable in service to Laban because he is **not** really a free man. Rebecca has sent him and she must send for him. Outlandish servitude is what he believes he deserves **not** because it is a reasonable arrangement with Laban, but because it is the unspoken penance for his crime against Esau. These seven years as "but a few days" are directly related to "the few days" that Rebecca prescribes as the interval of exile needed to assuage Esau's murderous wrath.

Jacob's deeply rooted sense of lack of entitlement also results in a strange but familiar response on his part to the later offer of Laban, "Name your wages and I will give them" (30:28). Toward the end of Jacob's twenty year stay in Laban's house, Laban has acknowledged his gratitude for Jacob's service and seems to be making a genuine offer. Yet, Jacob responds by saying, "Don't give me anything..." then proceeds to propose the famous and convoluted bargain wherein they will separate the speckled and spotted among the flocks, and divide the offspring on the basis of idiosyncratic

---

[5] The phrase appears only in these two verses in the entirety of the Hebrew Bible, besides an appearance in Daniel 11:20 (where the term seems to have nothing to do with the Jacob stories).

indicators in the next generation of sheep. The result of the entire complicated bargain (that entailed various manipulations by Jacob) was that Jacob gained possession of a great number of flocks (30:43).[6]

Not surprisingly, the text relates that this outcome (i.e., the new distribution of their father's wealth as a result of Jacob's manipulations), causes Jacob's brothers-in-law to resent him, ultimately making him flee:

> "And he heard the words of the sons of Laban saying, "Jacob has taken all of that which is our father's." (Gen. 31:1)

Thus, the emerging pattern entails a repetition of the earlier scenes wherein Jacob might have had the blessings of the paternal figure in a straightforward manner, but yet again, an inner compulsion leads him to achieve his desired goal through circuitous means—not unlike the means used in the taking of the birthright and the blessing. These means are perceived as devious and unjust by others and thereby resented by his brother/brothers-in-law even though there is a divine dream/promise to back up the result. In this repetition, the object of the deception is his father-in-law who now substitutes for Isaac the father. The outraged brothers-in-law substitute for the outraged brother, Esau. The result of the entire episode—yet again, Jacob must flee for his life.

Even in the "dream [or, prophetic] promises" that supposedly justify and call for the respective deceptions of both episodes, there is an idiosyncratic similarity. In the story of the speckled and spotted and striped sheep, Jacob seems to act on the basis of intuition and genetic manipulation. Only at the end of the story do we hear together with Rachel and Leah that the whole scheme was based on a prophetic dream. Only in 31:11—"an angel of the Lord appeared to me in a dream and said. . ."—does Jacob attribute

---

[6] The episode may have involved knowledge of the phenomenon we now refer to as "recessive genetic traits." See Yehuda Feliks, *Nature and Man in the Bible* (NY: Soncino Press, 1981) 9–13.

to the divine message of 31:3 ("... return to the land of your fathers") the additional instructions of how to manipulate the flocks. Jacob does not share in advance the divine "dream promise" with anyone, not even with his wives. As a direct result, he appears crafty and devious. This in turn, brings about the hatred of his brothers-in-law and Jacob's need to take flight. Similarly, it would seem that Rebecca never shared the prophetic vision of "the older will serve the younger" with Isaac or with anyone else.[7] As a result, she feels she must resort to devious means to procure the blessing for Jacob, which, in turn, brings about the hatred of Jacob's brother and Jacob's hasty flight to safety. It seems that like justice, divine will must be seen, as well as done. Or plainly stated, human action will be judged both by humanity and by God, not by how it dovetails with prophecy or with a pre-ordained divine will, but by the measure of universal moral standards.

Ultimately, in both cases, the engendered animosity threatens the physical welfare of Jacob and he is forced to flee. For our part, we will continue to explore the tense and often contradictory relationship between what the divine plan seems to be and the implicit condemnation of dubious human machinations to bring about the divinely mandated result.

The extraordinary parallel between this scene of the spotted, speckled, and streaked sheep, and the earlier scenes of exploitation, are further underscored by verse 30:37. There, Jacob's manipulations include taking the rods of various trees and "peeling **white** streaks in them, making the **white** within the rods appear..."

---

[7] The text itself back in Gen. 25:23 seems to highlight the fact that only Rebecca received the prophecy to the exclusion of Isaac. It does this by employing a rare syntactic construction "ויאמר י-הוה לה" with a sequence of a verb with the *vav* consecutive, followed by a proper noun, followed by the preposition "ל" with a suffix. Compare this to the more common construction as in Gen. 16:9, 10, 11. As Moshe Greenberg has pointed out, moving a word from its natural syntactic position in a sentence tends to emphasize the displaced word. It is my contention that here it produces the effect of "God spoke to *her*"; that is, not to *him*.

"וַיִּפְצֹל בָּהֵן פְּצָלוֹת **לְבָנוֹת** מַחְשֹׂף **הַלָּבָן**." This is done in manipulation of **לבן** Laban, whose name means "**white**." Recall that in the lentil soup scene, Jacob exploits the advantage of possessing the "**red, red** stuff" "**הָאָדֹם, הָאָדֹם הַזֶּה**" a story that leads to the exploited Esau being dubbed with the nickname **אֱדוֹם**—"**Red**."

Moreover, in the manipulation of the flocks, one type of sheep that Jacob aims to get is called streaked or "*bound with stripes*," in Hebrew "akudim"—**עֲקֻדִּים**. This term, "akud," cannot but take us back to the scene that has ever since been labeled "the *akeda*"—the *binding of Isaac*. "And Abraham built there an altar and *bound*—**וַיַּעֲקֹד**—Isaac his son" (Gen. 22:9). The grammatical form of "akudim" is passive, thus if referring back to Moriah, it is a reference to Isaac, not to Abraham. Jacob, again, resorts to manipulation to gain possession of the blessing of "*the bound*," symbolically—the blessing of the unattainable love of the father still *bound* to the altar.

There are still further indications that the subtext of Jacob's sojourn in Laban's house is intricately tied to his earlier doings and to the repressed moral conscience of Jacob knocking on the cellar door. Again, these indications make themselves known through the curious surface ripples that occur when there is an odd or "wrong" or inordinately repeated choice of words.

In the story of Jacob's flight from Laban—a departure secretly undertaken while Laban is off on his (annual?) sheep shearing trip—the term **גנב**, *to steal*, is used repeatedly in an unusually concentrated stretch of text (Gen. 31:19–39):

יט) וְלָבָן הָלַךְ לִגְזֹז אֶת צֹאנוֹ וַתִּ**גְנֹב** רָחֵל אֶת הַתְּרָפִים אֲשֶׁר לְאָבִיהָ

כ) וַיִּ**גְנֹב** יַעֲקֹב אֶת לֵב לָבָן הָאֲרַמִּי עַל בְּלִי הִגִּיד לוֹ כִּי בֹרֵחַ הוּא

כו) וַיֹּאמֶר לָבָן לְיַעֲקֹב מֶה עָשִׂיתָ וַתִּ**גְנֹב** אֶת לְבָבִי וַתְּנַהֵג אֶת בְּנֹתַי כִּשְׁבֻיוֹת חָרֶב

כז) לָמָּה נַחְבֵּאתָ לִבְרֹחַ וַתִּ**גְנֹב** אֹתִי וְלֹא הִגַּדְתָּ לִּי וָאֲשַׁלֵּחֲךָ

98

בְּשִׂמְחָה...

ל) וְעַתָּה הָלֹךְ הָלַכְתָּ כִּי נִכְסֹף נִכְסַפְתָּה לְבֵית אָבִיךְ לָמָּה **גָנַבְתָּ** אֶת אֱלֹהָי

לא) וַיַּעַן יַעֲקֹב וַיֹּאמֶר לְלָבָן כִּי יָרֵאתִי כִּי אָמַרְתִּי פֶּן **תִּגְזֹל**[8] אֶת בְּנוֹתֶיךָ מֵעִמִּי

לב) עִם אֲשֶׁר תִּמְצָא אֶת אֱלֹהֶיךָ לֹא יִחְיֶה נֶגֶד אַחֵינוּ הַכֶּר לְךָ מָה עִמָּדִי וְקַח לָךְ וְלֹא יָדַע יַעֲקֹב כִּי רָחֵל **גְּנָבָתַם**...

לט) טְרֵפָה לֹא הֵבֵאתִי אֵלֶיךָ אָנֹכִי אֲחַטֶּנָּה מִיָּדִי תְּבַקְשֶׁנָּה **גְּנֻבְתִי** יוֹם וּ**גְנֻבְתִי** לָיְלָה

19) ...and Rachel **stole** the teraphim of her father...

20) And Jacob **stole** the heart of Laban the Aramean by not telling him that he was fleeing...

26) And Laban said to Jacob, "what have you done that you have **stolen** my heart and led off my daughters like captives of the sword?"

27) "Why have you secretly run off, **stealing** me...

30) ...Why have you **stolen** my gods?"

31) And Jacob answered and said to Laban, "because I was afraid you would **steal**[9] your daughters from me."

32) "The one with whom you shall find your gods shall not live..." and Jacob did not know that Rachel had **stolen** them.

39) "[of any casualties among the flocks I tended] I bore the loss... whether **stolen** by day or **stolen** by night."

This text, illustrating the well known technique termed by Buber and Rosenzweig—the *Leitwort*, or repeated use of a key word or phrase in order to underscore the central theme of a passage—points to the central

---

[8] *Gazol* is a different verb than the other eight appearances of ganov, but it carries an almost identical meaning.

[9] See previous note.

motif of our story. A man—whose life is not his own—sees himself and is seen by others as having stolen even that which rightfully belongs to him. Even the right to one's wives or children, and even the basic right to quit a place of work or to return to one's home, are seen as the property or prerogative of others. I am, of course, suggesting yet again that the theme of *measure for measure*, which has been amply demonstrated as a key to the Jacob narratives, has resonated once more.

The *stolen* birthright and blessing have deprived Jacob not only of his own sense of entitlement, but also of Laban's (and the narrative voice's) perception of Jacob as owner of his own life. He has *stolen* Laban's heart as clearly as Rachel has *stolen* the household gods (31:20). Acts that could have been perceived as reclaiming his life are seen as stealing. Until Jacob can come face to face *(panim el panim)* and wrestle with what he has done to his standing with his fellow man and to his standing with God, he will live in a state of dissociation and dispossession.[10] Jacob cannot possess that which is Jacob's until he ceases becoming the other. The pattern—of relinquishing his identity and his moral autonomy to Rebecca, Esau, Laban, or even to God (as in the vow)—places Jacob's family and his possessions in perpetual mortgage.

Particularly telling in this regard is not only the repeated occurrence of the word *stolen,* but its idiosyncratic use in verse thirty-nine (above). The Hebrew word גנבתי pronounced *"genuvti"* is unique in the Bible and is presumed by Rashi and by moderns to be a rare, archaic, poetic grammatical form of *"genuvat"* (literally: stolen of).[11] Indeed, if we read

---

[10] See Gen. 32:31 and the entire episode of the Jabok river crossing which will be analyzed in detail in the coming pages.

[11] This interpretation of the *ti* ending of *genuvti* relies on its similarity to the word *"rabati"* in Lamentations 1:1. The ancient Aramaic translation of Onkelos renders the meaning in context of *genuvti* as *my guarding [from being stolen]*. This solves the issue of the *"ti"* ending to the word that would now mean as it usually does—"my"; this, without resorting to archaic poetic forms. The other school of thought was forced into interpreting the *"ti"* ending so unusually because they could not account for its meaning as *"my stealing."* After all, Jacob here is defending himself, not incriminating

the word with the same letters, but supply it with different vocalization, *genuvti* becomes *ganavti*—literally: "I stole." If we are open and attentive to the possibility of parapraxis, we would not at all be surprised to find Jacob defending himself with words that could be construed, vocalized or simply heard as self-incrimination. Regardless of how various exegetes solve the unique word form, we must still inquire as to why a man who wants to say "my guarding [from being stolen]" winds up saying the equivalent of "my stealing" instead.

Moreover, the only other use of the grammatical form *genuv* or *ganuv* (in this particular passive form) in the Bible is earlier in this same story (30:33).[12] There, Jacob anticipates Laban's possible objection to the consequences of the division of the spotted and non-spotted sheep, by saying, "if you find the wrong colored sheep in my flock, you will know it is *ganuv* [stolen]." Here is a classic instance of a man who—prior to being accused or suspected—invites incrimination by *protesting too much* his innocence. Jacob has the term *ganov* on the brain and on the lips; at times the word sneaks into his language in ways so unusual or inappropriate as to have generations of exegetes searching for resolution.

Aside from the repeated appearance of the verb "to steal," there are two other phrases that recur several times in the passage quoted above—"to flee" and "to tell" (or more precisely "*not* telling"). Most notably, all three

himself! Yet Onkelos' translation is a highly reasonable interpretation considering the occasional occurrence of metonymy in biblical language, wherein words that denote cause and result or other closely related concepts are often interchanged. Nonetheless, whether we accept Onkelos' or Rashi's explanation of "*genuvti,*" we are hard pressed to account for the strange usage, particularly the suffix "*ti*" which normatively would be understood as denoting "*my*" stealing.

[12] A similar but not identical occurrence can be found in Genesis 40:15. Joseph: "I was stolen, yes stolen (*"gunov gunavti"*), from the land of the Hebrews." Is this nuanced description of the kidnapping of Jacob's favored son yet another subtle literary indicator of the *measure for measure* retribution for Jacob's sins?—thus, accounting for the doubling of the verb and the passive form in both verses, *genuvti, genuvti* 31:39, and *gunov gunavti* 40:15. See further comments on this parallel in the coming pages.

terms are used together in both verses 20 and 27:

> "And Jacob **stole** the heart of Laban the Aramean in **not telling** him that he was **fleeing**." (31:20)

> "Why have you secretively **fled**, you have **stolen** me, **not telling** me...." (31:27)

It seems that the modus operandi of Jacob involves fleeing (evasion) and deception that manifests itself in an inability "to tell." Language, however, particularly when trying to conceal, has a way of revealing through subtext precisely those evasions or repressions that are not directly told. Indeed, the confluence of odd or anomalous word choices in the verses describing Laban's confrontation with the fleeing Jacob points to a very rich subtext. The narrative may stress Jacob's *not telling,* but its language and intertextual references are extremely *telling.*

Consider, to begin with, Laban's words to Jacob in verse 31:28:

ולא נטשתני לנשק לבני ולבנתי עתה הסכלת עשו

The text seems to be manipulating Laban's words as well as Jacob's in order to refer both Jacob and the reader back to the scene of the deception. In these words of Laban—"You have not even *let me kiss* **my son**s and daughters, and now you have indeed been foolish in action" (Gen. 31:28)— there are two words used with either anomalous form or anomalous connotation respectively. The reader is struck by the words לא נטשתני—*lo netashtani* to mean "you have not *allowed*" (or "*let*"), as the word *natash* never means this elsewhere in the Bible, but rather to *abandon* or to *forsake,* often used in the context of forsaking one's (*nachala*) inheritance.[13]

---

[13] See Jeremiah 12:7, II Kings 21:14, I Samuel 12:22, Psalms 94:14. Only in this verse according to Even-Shoshan does the word mean to *let* or to *allow.*

Moreover, the rare appearance of the form of the verb עשה—"*to do*" in the infinitive (translated above as action)—almost never appears elsewhere with the spelling עשו *(aso)*—identical to (and only vocalized differently from) the Hebrew for Esau.[14] If one connects these two anomalous uses of language in the context of a father kissing his children to the mental image of Isaac calling Jacob close to be kissed as Esau (Gen. 27:26–27), there is yet another element of the deception that is brought to Jacob's subconscious by analogy. Jacob *kisses* as עשו *Esau, in order not to forsake* the blessing or inheritance. Kissing in the deception scene is the closest and most intimate element of Jacob's masquerade, and therefore the most painful to recollect, and the most prone to resistance.[15]

The moment of the kiss as a key element in the deception of the blind Isaac is further underscored and echoed at the end of Genesis when Jacob, himself now blind, had Joseph *bring close* Jacob's grandchildren and *he kissed them.* The very same combination of verbs is used twice in Gen. 27:27—"***Come close** and **kiss** me my son, and he **came close** and **kissed** him* גשה נא ושקה לי בני **ויגש וישק** לו"—and in 48:10: *"and Israel's (Jacob's) eyes were heavy with age, he could not see, and he had them **come close** to him and he **kissed** them....* "ועיני ישראל כבדו מזקן לא יוכל לראות **ויגש** אתם אליו **וישק** להם.

In the next two verses of Laban's speech, hidden within the words, there

---

[14] See the notes in *Biblia Hebraica* to Gen. 31:28 that record the variant Samaritan text of *asoth* (עשות). Clearly, the suggestion of an intertextual illusion becomes moot if one adopts this version of the word. If however the anomalous spelling עשו is retained, the Samaritan text can be seen as an attempt by a scribe to consciously or unconsciously copy the more common word. See Timpanaro's theory of *banalization* mentioned earlier—Introduction, note 10.

[15] The word *"hiskalta"* (you have done foolishly), in the context of deceiving a father, further connects with the similar word *"sikel"* which means to switch or cross [hands] which is used in the scene in which the blind Jacob purposely switches the older son of Joseph with the younger. This might give additional credence to a reading that attributes wordplay at hand in using the word for Esau (עשו) in a verse describing Jacob's deception of Laban. It is yet another way of pointing to the subtext of Jacob's deception of his father that runs through the scenes with Jacob's father-in-law.

is further intertextual wordplay sending us back to the deception scene:

כט) "יֶשׁ לְאֵל **יָדִי** לַ**עֲשׂוֹת** עִמָּכֶם רָע **וֵאלֹהֵי אֲבִיכֶם אֶמֶשׁ** אָמַר אֵלַי לֵאמֹר הִשָּׁמֶר לְךָ מִ**דַּבֵּר** עִם **יַעֲקֹב** מִטּוֹב עַד רָע

ל) וְעַתָּה הָלֹךְ הָלַכְתָּ כִּי **נִכְסֹף נִכְסַפְתָּה** לְבֵית אָבִיךָ לָמָּה **גָנַבְתָּ** אֶת אֱלֹהָי"

> "It is within the power of **my hand to deal** with you badly but the God of your fathers told me last night saying: be careful not to be **speaking with Jacob** well or badly. Now you have gone and went because you longed greatly for your father's house. 'Why have you stolen my gods?'" (Gen. 31:29–30)

Within the words for "my power [literally: 'hand'] to deal" (*yadi laasot*) are the Hebrew letters that spell ידי עשו—"the hands of Esau." Juxtaposed with Laban's "power to deal badly" in the second part of the verse is a reference to "speaking with Jacob," an apposition that reminds us of Isaac's puzzlement—"the voice is the voice of Jacob but the hands are the hands of Esau" (Gen. 27:22). Once again, we are reminded of Jacob's choice of words in fearfully asking for God's help against the "**hands of Esau**" (Gen. 32:12).

In the middle of this same verse, the words "God of your father last night"—א-להי אביכם אמש—contain the Hebrew letters that comprise Jacob's temporary hesitation in the deception scene—**אולי ימשני אבי**—perhaps my father will feel me."[16] (Further play on the

---

[16] The word אמש (last night) is related to the word in Arabic and in other Semitic languages for darkness. It is entirely possible that the word משש (to feel or grope in the dark) belongs to a common etymology, though the word play suggested will neither be confirmed nor ruled out by the accuracy of the etymological suggestion. The word אמש only appears five times in the Hebrew Bible; according to Concordance Even-Shoshan the word means "darkness" in Job 30:3. This possible etymological

theme of feeling or groping, משש, is evident in the continuation of this scene of confrontation between Jacob and Laban with the repeated appearance of the verb משש in an anomalous context.)

The following verse, *you longed greatly for your father's house*, twice uses the Hebrew word כסף *(kesef)* as a verb meaning "to long for." It is the only place in the five books of Moses in which this word means "to long for"—seemingly unrelated to the common meaning of the word כסף as "money" or "silver." Is there a hidden reference or implication that Jacob's separation from (and longing for) his father's home is related to a fleeing on account of money? "...הלך הלכת כי נכסף נכספת." One might suggest that the text describing Jacob's "longing for father's house" using uncommon words that connote "money" has to do with a subtext of Jacob having stolen the material blessing of Isaac's wealth. Certainly, the suggestion of double entendre here is supported by the complaint of Jacob's wives fifteen verses earlier (Gen. 31:15). Rachel and Leah had agreed to Jacob's plan to finally leave their father's house after twenty years because in any case Laban "has devoured our dowry"—"כספנו". Moreover, this notion is bolstered by the surprise ending of this verse—". . . you have longed for your father's house, why have you stolen my gods?" In fact, when one considers the extensive literary parallel between this scene in which Rachel steals the gods of Laban and the later scene in which Joseph the son of Rachel plants a cup of *silver* (כסף) in the sack of Rachel's other son Benjamin, there is further support to the idea of נכסף נכספת—*nikhsof nikhsafta*—as word play for *kesef* (money or silver).

In our introductory chapter, we discussed the idea that words can mean one thing in their contextual frame and yet still point to an intertextual referent wherein the words mean something else entirely—a phenomenon that has been termed "syllepsis." At this point it will be useful to recall the assertion that an intentional use of syllepsis is particularly indicated when

relationship would also resonate in Exodus 10:21, where God brings upon Egypt the plague of a "darkness that is felt—וימש חשך".

the use of a word or phrase in its contextual meaning is exceedingly rare—
as in the cases of "*nikhsafta*" and "*aso*" and "*emesh*" and "*yad Esav.*"

Returning to the beginning of the "*genuvti*" verse, we encounter another odd choice of words. When Jacob tells Laban with regard to the
cases of missing sheep, "אנכי אחטנה" (*anokhi achatena*)—which we have
translated together with JPS and others as, "I bore the loss" or "I made
good the loss"—the translation has also masked an anomalous use of the
word אחטנה *achatena*. According to Abraham Even Shoshan's Biblical
Concordance, the verb root חטא *chato* appears two hundred and thirty-
eight times in the Bible; only here in this verse does the word mean *to give
recompense* or *to bear the loss*. Most entries (where the word appears in the
kal form) bear the meaning of the root חטא as to *sin*. Here again, though
the translation is contextually warranted and etymologically defensible,[17]
one is left to ponder why yet again Jacob uses highly unusual language in
which the wordplay is suggestive of sin (חטא) or self incrimination—אנכי
אחטנה—in a speech proclaiming his honesty to Laban.

There is psychological coherence to the timing of these surface ripples
that indicate the lurking presence of unresolved, repressed guilt. Having
used dubious—even though divinely coordinated—means of getting his
father-in-law's wealth, Jacob has provoked his **brothers-in-law's** hatred
to the point of having to flee. In this sequence, Jacob is clearly returning to
the scene of chapter 27, where after using duplicitous means to acquire his
father's blessing, thereby provoking his **brother's** hatred, he is forced to
flee. He is, if only through his unconscious experience as indicated by his

---

[17] The grammatical *pi'el* form of the word here could be seen as reflecting the
infrequent but bona fide secondary meaning of *chato* as *to bring a sacrificial offering
in recompense for something that should have occurred but was missing*. Thus, making a
gift of sheep in order to replace missing sheep, both fits the context of Jacob's words to
Laban and more loosely the context in which the term is used in sacrificial passages.
The *piel* form of the verb is also sometimes used to mean *purge*. Nonetheless, the
specific form and usage in Gen. 31: 39 with the contextual meaning of *to bear the
loss* remains unique and problematic.

FIVE: IN LABAN'S HOUSE

odd choice of language, reliving his earlier sins and the resulting repression of guilt. Of course, the psychological frame of causality may be said to run simultaneously in both directions. The repetition of a similar situation takes one's unconscious back to the earlier scene and at the same time, it is the unresolved nature of the earlier episode that *compels* one to arrive at repetition. In fact, one might venture the following formulation: The *present* so closely echoes the past because it is the past that has arranged its own *presentation* at our doorstep.

Once one sees in Jacob's words to Laban a subtext that points back to Jacob's repressed need to confront his own deception of his father and brother, one is tempted to see the entire verse upon which we have been focusing, as text and subtext:

"טרפה לא הבאתי אליך אנכי אחטנה מידי תבקשנה גנבתי יום וגנבתי לילה"

> "I have not brought you prey [of beasts], I [sinned] bore the loss, from my hand you requested it, stolen by day, stolen by night."

On the level of simple context, Jacob is defending his unassailable honesty as shepherd of Laban's flocks to his father-in-law. Our verse is parallel to Exodus 22:12, where the law is set down that if the lamb or other animal of one's neighbor in your keep is "torn, torn to pieces—אם טרף יטרף יביאהו עד הטרפה לא ישלם—he is to bring the prey as evidence, what was torn he does not have to pay back."[18] In other words, there are cases where the sheep under one's watch are lost because of circumstances beyond the control of even the most conscientious of shepherds, and as a result—the shepherd is absolved of responsibility for the loss. Jacob is thus telling Laban that he never utilized this exemption as Laban

---

[18] This was apparently a commonly held practice encapsulated by legal dicta throughout the ancient Near East, as evidenced by Hammurabi Code, paragraph 226, as well as by Exodus 22:12.

would have asked him to pay anyway. He replaced the livestock whether eaten by wild animals, or stolen by day or night.

On the level of subtext, however, if one substitutes father for father-in-law, and context of self-vindication with repressed self-incrimination, the resulting alternative meaning of his words reads, remarkably, as follows: "I have not brought you prey [the venison requested of Esau, but rather the goats prepared by Rebecca],[19] I, אנכי (*anokhi*—the same word for "I" that Jacob used when he said to Isaac *"anokhi Esau," "I am Esau")* have sinned, from my hand you asked for it [for the venison, see 27:25], stolen by day, stolen by night." (This is perhaps a subconscious allusion to the deception that exploited the darkness of Isaac's blindness, hence, "stolen in broad daylight which to you was night.")

The following chart will clarify the subtle relationship between text and subtext. In each part of these verses there will be instances of syllepsis—wherein words will be understood one way in context and in another way as intertextual links to the deception scene. At times, the subtext will be suggested by an uncontextually literal translation as well:

---

[19] Support for substituting the term *"terefa"* (literally: *torn of beasts,* but liberally translated here as *prey*) for the *"tz-d"* (literally: *hunt)* of Esau (also translated liberally here as *prey*) may be found in verses in which *"teref" is used generally to* mean food. See Malakhi 3:10, Psalms 111:5, and Proverbs 31:15. Even stronger and more idiosyncratic support is suggested by the use of *"teref"* in Job 38:39, which reads: "Can you **hunt prey** for the lion?" התצוד ללביא טרף"—Ha-ta-**tzud. . . teref**." Here the object of a human *hunt* is called *teref.*

Genesis 31:38–39	Genesis 27	Genesis 31:38–39	
CONTEXTUAL TRANSLATION	INTERTEXTUAL REFERENCES	SUBTEXT	בראשית לא: לח-לט
"… thy **she-goats** have not become **bereft of offspring**; your **sheep** I have not **eaten**	Rebecca to Jacob: Go now to the **sheep** (צאן) and fetch for me from there two good kids of **she-goats** (עזים) and **bring** them to your father that he may **eat**. … Why should I be **bereft** of the two of you.	*Your* flocks have not had she-goats go missing	...רחליך לא שכלו ואילי צאנך לא אכֿ לתי...
Torn of beasts (**prey**) I have not **brought** you	"hunt me some **prey**… and **bring** it to me" (Isaac to Esau in Gen. 27:3–4). Rebecca has Jacob substitute she-goats from the flock to serve in lieu of Esau's prey.	I didn't bring you prey as I did to Isaac when I brought the she-goats from his flock disguised as prey (venison).	טרפה לא הבאתי אליך
I *(anokhi)* bore the loss of it—**achatena**	"I *(anokhi)* am Esau your first-born." (Jacob to Isaac, Gen. 27:19) this statement = the essence of the sin of deceit	I *(anokhi)* have sinned —**achatena** (by saying *anokhi?*) "bore the loss" is a contextual translation.	אנכי אחטנה
You requested it [the prey] from my hand	"and he knew him not for his hands were hairy… and he said serve me [the venison (prey)]" (Isaac to Jacob masquerading as Esau in Gen. 27:23–5)	You (Isaac substituting for Laban) requested it [the prey]. From my **hand** (essence of the ruse = "the **hands** are the hands of Esau")	מידי תבקשנה
Whether stolen by day or by night	And Isaac's eyes were dim so that he could not see…. (Gen. 27:1) "Your brother has come in deceit and taken your blessing." (Gen. 27:35)	My having stolen in daylight—night [to the blind Isaac]	גנבתי יום וגנבתי לילה
Import: I (Jacob) have acted above and beyond the accepted standards of fairness and loyalty to my father-in-law in my dealings		Import: I (Jacob) have descended beneath all standards of fairness and loyalty to my brother and loyalty to my father in my dealings	

What is the literary significance of using language that creates multiple associations with Jacob's deception of his father in a dialogue in which Jacob's father-in-law accuses him of "stealing his heart." On the one hand, we witness here an extensive use of irony. Yet, on the other hand, we might also see in these parallels the intimations of a repressed moral discomfort on the part of Jacob who reacts unconsciously—and thus, with vehement overreaction—to the accusations of Laban and to the mental associations they trigger.

Whichever the case, it is even more apparent that these verses in Jacob's conversation with Laban point forward (as well as back in time) and resonate in the language used to describe the later (*measure for measure*) separation from his own son(s):

> Jacob says to Laban: "the she-goats from your flock have not miscarried שכלו [*shikelu*—literally: to become **bereft of offspring**], I have not *eaten* (אכלתי) the rams from your flock, **torn by beasts טרפה, I have not brought you. . . you have requested it from my hands, stolen גנבתי by day, stolen גנבתי by night.**"

> רְחֵלֶיךָ וְעִזֶּיךָ לֹא **שִׁכֵּלוּ** וְאֵילֵי צֹאנְךָ לֹא **אָכָלְתִּי**
> **טְרֵפָה לֹא הֵבֵאתִי** אֵלֶיךָ אָנֹכִי אֲחַטֶּנָּה מִיָּדִי תְּבַקְשֶׁנָּה **גְּנֻבְתִי** יוֹם **וּגְנֻבְתִי**
> לָיְלָה (Gen. 31:38–39)

He later tells his own sons of his anguish at the (false) news of Joseph's death:

> "A terrible beast has *eaten* him (אכלתהו), Joseph is *torn, torn to pieces!* (טרף טרף)." (Gen. 37:33)

Later, in reference to the loss of sons:

*"As I **am bereft**, so will I be **bereft**—כאשר שכלתי שכלתי."* (Gen. 43:14)

And again, in the context of Judah trying to receive Jacob's permission to risk Benjamin, the narration uses Jacob's earlier words to Laban (this time in the mouth of Judah):

"From my hands you will request him [it]—מידי תבקשנו, if **I will not have brought** him back לא הביאותיו". (Gen. 43:9)

Moreover, the double expression of ***genuvti, genuvti*** is later echoed by the text when Joseph describes himself as having been "**stolen, yes stolen**, from the land of the Hebrews"—***gunov gunavti*** *me'eretz ha'ivrim.* (Gen. 40:15)

Again, the parallel language and content—that describe both Jacob's defense against Laban's accusations as well as the future loss of Jacob's own son Joseph (through the deception of Joseph's brothers)—might best be summarized by the following chart:

Jacob to Laban (Gen. 31:38-9)	Jacob's loss of Joseph
רחליך ועזיך "Your ewes and your **she-goats**	וישחטו שעיר עזים "And they slaughtered a kid of the **she-goats** and dipped the coat in the blood" (Gen. 37:32)
לא שכלו Have not miscarried (*shikelu*—**become bereft**)	ואני כאשר שכלתי, שכלתי "If I **become bereft** of children, then I will be **bereft**" (Gen. 43:14)—Jacob becoming resigned to the possible loss of Benjamin as he has for Joseph, Benjamin's brother.

Jacob to Laban (Gen. 31:38-9)	Jacob's loss of Joseph
ואילי צאנך לא **אכלתי** And the rams of your flock I have not **eaten**	חיה רעה **אכלתהו** A wild beast has **eaten** him (Gen. 37:33)
טרפה Torn of beasts—*terefa*	**טרף טרף** יוסף Joseph has been **torn, torn** [**by beasts**]. (Gen. 37:33)
לא **הבאתי** אליך I have **not brought you.** I bore the loss of it אנכי (**אחטנה**) *(achatena)* **מידי תבקשנה** from my **hand you demanded it** *miyadi tevakshena*	"**מידי תבקשנה** אם לא הביאותיו אליך **וחטאתי** לך כל הימים" ". . . from my **hand you will demand** **him** (*miyadi tevakshena*) if I will **not have** **brought him** to you. . . and I will have **sinned** (*chatati*—same root as *achatena*) against you all my days." (Gen. 43:9)
גנבתי יום, **גנבתי** לילה Whether **stolen** by day or **stolen** by night *Genuvti yom, genuvti leila.*	כי **גנב גנבתי** מארץ העברים I was **stolen**, yes **stolen**, from the land of the Hebrews (Gen. 40:15) Joseph to his cellmate in prison

Language and subtext are used in the passage describing Jacob's encounter with Laban so as to connect the present not only with the past but also with the future—just as surely as life's "subtexts" resonate with the past, they inform the future.

Yet, there is still more evidence here of Jacob's psychological return to the deception scene. In verses thirty-six and thirty-seven, Jacob expresses great umbrage at the audacity of Laban's searching his tents for his household gods. Note the language used to describe his outrage:

"What is my crime פשעי, what is my sin חטאתי, that you have lit after me and *groped* משׁשׁת through all my vessels. . . ?"

What crime, indeed? What sin? And here the text becomes so inter-textually explicit as to nearly answer the rhetorical question of Jacob. The feeling or groping of his father-in-law is at once a reference and a response to his father's feeling and groping. The verb משׁשׁ—(*to grope* or *to feel*)—already used by the narration in verse 34 to describe Laban's intrusive and suspicious search, is only used in one other context in the book of Genesis. When Isaac is suspicious of Jacob, he calls him to come closer so that "I may *feel you* ואמשׁך, to know if you are indeed Esau my son or not" (Gen. 27:21–22). We have already commented on Jacob's concern, *"perhaps* my father will *feel me"*—"אולי ימשׁני אבי" (Gen. 27:12). In fact, this use of the word משׁשׁ—to describe Laban's feeling or groping—conforms perfectly to the pattern of anomalous language, and of tellingly odd or "wrong" word choice. Every other appearance of the word משׁשׁ in the Bible, including the appearances in the deception scene, are cases of blind people "groping" or of a seeing person "groping" or "feeling his way" in darkness. Only in the case of Laban has the word been chosen to describe the groping of a seeing person in daytime.[20]

The anomalous word choice does not surprise us though, for its inter-textual payload is as obvious as it is effective. The father-in-law Laban's suspicion of theft transports both Jacob and the reader back to the scene of father Isaac's suspicion of theft. Thus, the language used by Jacob to describe Laban's search becomes the borrowed terminology from the earlier scene, however inappropriate in the present context. Psychologically,

---

[20] The text could easily have used the root חפשׂ (to search) instead of משׁשׁ (to grope or feel), as indeed it does in the very next verse (Gen. 31:35). In fact, the phrase ". . . he groped. . . but did not find" in verse 34 is paraphrased in verse 35, where it reads ". . . he searched. . . but did not find."

as Laban the father-in-law substitutes for Isaac the father, the feeling and groping triggers a self justifying response: "What is my crime and what is my sin?"

There is one more curious expression that tragically makes its way from Jacob's troubled subconscious into his parapraxis ridden vocabulary. When protesting his innocence and that of his family, Jacob tells Laban: "I was afraid you would steal your daughters from me—[yet another expression that combines stealing and Jacob's own sense that his entitlement does not even extend to his wives whom he calls Laban's daughters]—with whomsoever you shall find your gods, [such person] **shall not live**... and Jacob knew not that Rachel had stolen them" (Gen. 31:31–32). The pronouncement, of course, becomes prophetically true, as Rachel dies soon thereafter in childbirth.[21] Jacob has unwittingly issued a death sentence on his beloved wife for a crime (theft) that does not warrant the ultimate punishment.[22] What is it about the very suspicion of theft that drives Jacob to the overheated response and tragic slip of tongue that literally reads, "[one who steals] **cannot [or shall not] live**"?[23] Substitute Isaac for Laban in Jacob's unconscious transference, the suspicion of theft of gods for that of blessings, and the subtext of his overreaction becomes obvious. The shadow and echoed repetition of **theft**—and its consequent cycle of suspicion, hatred, and fleeing from family—are unbearable burdens with which Jacob **cannot live**.

---

[21] The context of her death further connects her to idol-worship and specifically to the *teraphim* (household gods) as she names the child born as she dies in childbirth *Ben Oni* בן אוני. David Silber has noted the connection in various biblical texts between *teraphim* and *On* און. See I Samuel 15: 23, and Zechariah 10:2.

[22] It is clear from the context that the crime alluded to is theft and not idol worship. Though later in the Bible, idol worship warrants the death penalty, in pre-Sinai narratives this is not the case, as is explicit in Genesis 35:2–4, where Jacob himself instructs his household members to rid themselves of "foreign gods." There, the only consequence is the need for the offenders to purify themselves and change their clothing.

[23] The Hebrew *lo yihye* can mean *shall not, will not,* or *cannot live.*

CHAPTER SIX

PREPARATIONS FOR TRANSITION:
GEOGRAPHY AS PSYCHOLOGICAL TERRITORY

As Jacob proceeds from his confrontation with Laban he is met by angels
of the Lord (Gen. 32:1-3). The Hebrew word for *met* here is the verb פגע—a
word rarely used with this meaning—that takes us back to Jacob's previous
fleeing where he had encountered ויפגע (more literally: *bumped into*) the
place where he dreamed of angels ascending and descending. Here too,
as in the case of Beth-El, he is inspired by the vision of angels to name the
place. This time he regards the site of his vision not as a "house of the Lord
and a gateway to heaven" but as an "encampment of the Lord," *Machane
Elohim,* and he calls it *Machanaim*, which means "two camps."[1] Presumably, "the two camps" is a reference to both the human encampment

---

[1] Moshe Greenberg has called to my attention that the *"a'im"* suffix that usually
means *two*, sometimes appears without that connotation when referring to a place,
as in Yerushala*'im*. Nonetheless, here in the case of *machna'im*, we have cause to
see its meaning as *two camps*, particularly in light of the appearance of the explicit
use of the phrase *two camps* up ahead in 32:8 and again in 32:11.

of Jacob and the divine encampment of the Lord.[2] Clearly, this brief and cryptic scene is a foreshadowing of the dramatic scene later in this chapter that ends by describing Jacob as having "struggled with *divinities (Elohim)* and with men." It is also the first of several dualities or dichotomies invoked by Jacob that speak of his situation as bifurcated.

Jacob sends messengers—in Hebrew, **malakhim**, the same word for angels—to Esau and they return with word that Esau is approaching with a war party of four hundred men. Jacob then divides (ויחץ) his people in half, creating two camps—**machanot** (Gen. 32:11). He then turns to God, the Lord of his fathers, and describes his situation as having changed from the lonely traveler with only a staff in hand, to the man who has "become *two camps—machanot*" (Gen. 32:12). Taken literally, this latter verse is particularly striking, as it is not his family or entourage, but Jacob himself who has become "*two camps*"— הייתי לשני מחנות.

We shall see this theme of bifurcation reach its climax at the river crossing where Jacob seems to split *himself* into two, in order to wrestle with himself. Genesis 32:24, introducing the struggle at the Jabok crossing, implies the concept of wrestling with self by stating, "*Va-yivater Yaakov l'vado (and Jacob remained alone), vayeavek ish imo (and a man wrestled with him).*" If one does not read the two phrases as sequential but as simultaneous, the only way for Jacob to be alone and yet wrestling with another would be if the "other" is the other half of Jacob.

This interpretation—of wrestling with self—would also account for the answer of the mysterious wrestler to Jacob's request in 32:30, "Pray, tell me your name." The stranger answers, "why indeed should you ask my name?" This might be taken to mean, *you already know perfectly well who I am*! It has long occurred to me that the term in Hebrew for *remained alone—vayevater* is very nearly an aural homonym for yet another word—

---

[2] See Nachmanides, Seforno, and other commentaries to Genesis 32:3.

(besides ויחץ)—that also means to bifurcate—ויבתר, *vayevater*.[3]

There is another crucial and symbol laden scene in which the protagonist is described as *l'vado*—**alone**—with the parallel lending further credence to the reading here of Jacob split in two. In the passage in chapter two of Genesis, Adam is also subdivided in order to be rejoined and become a whole greater than prior to his bifurcation. Before the creation of woman, Adam is seen as lacking wholeness—*lo tov heyot haAdam l'vado* (*it is not good for man to be* **alone**), Gen. 2:18.

The similarity extends beyond the need to paradoxically achieve wholeness through becoming two, as there is a remarkable use of parallel language. In order for Adam to make way for Eve, God causes slumber to fall upon Adam and takes from him one of his ribs. The word for *rib* in Hebrew is צלע (**tzela**) which most often in the Bible means "a side." In fact, various midrashic interpretations draw upon the double meaning of *tzela* and prefer to see Adam split in two (a whole **side** taken from him), rather than the conventional understanding of *tzela* as "rib."

Tzela is also the root of the verb—צלע—"to limp" (to walk favoring *one side*).[4] The process of Adam becoming whole is achieved at the cost of his *tzela*. The price Jacob pays for the bifurcation and wrestling with self at Jabok—the injury that will make him whole[5] in the sense of achieving integrity—is his limping away (צולע—*tzolea*) from the encounter.[6]

---

[3] See Genesis 15:10, where Abraham bifurcates (*vayevater*) various animals in the "covenant of the pieces." I would be more hesitant to suggest the presence of audial wordplay were it not for the other clear instances of such punning and the cumulative effect of such in this chapter, Gen. 32.

[4] Though historically these words (*tzela* as rib or side and *tzolea* to limp) may come from different roots, as indicated by cognate languages, the relevant consonants may have coalesced in Hebrew. My thanks go to Bob Brody for pointing this out. In any case, the use of these words with identical lettering—as intertextually connecting two passages—may be true irrespective of historical etymology.

[5] See Genesis 33:18: "And Jacob came *shalem* [complete] to the city of Shechem."

[6] Both the similar language of *l'vado* and that of *tzela* have been noted in Leon Kass, *The Beginning of Wisdom: Reading Genesis* (NY: Free Press, 2003), pages 455

Before approaching the passage at Jabok, we must note two other literary techniques employed previously in the buildup toward that scene. As others have noted, two key terms repeated in rapid succession in the preparation of Jacob for his long dreaded encounter with Esau, are the roots אחר *a-h-r* and פנה *p-n-h.* The root אחר—in its various forms and meanings—means to *tarry,* to *be behind, after,* or *in back of.* It is related to at least one of the meanings of the name Jacob (יעקב) as the root עקב means the **back** side of the foot or the "**heel** that trails **behind**." The root פנה in its various constructions may mean *face,* or *to face,* or *in front of* or *before.* The coming scene will indeed reflect the transition of Jacob from a figure who continuously *sneaks* away or *comes from behind,* to one who con*fronts face to face.*

Seen as a struggle not just with Esau, but primarily with himself, the scene at Jabok will deal with Jacob finally forsaking his various *circumventions* (another meaning of his name) and coming to terms with his own identity face to face.

In his first deployment of envoys to Esau, Jacob bids the messengers to say to him, "Thus sayeth your brother Jacob, 'I have dwelt with Laban and have *tarried* (ואחר) until now.'" Rather than speak of his hasty flight from Esau's murderous wrath and his twenty year refuge in Laban's house, Jacob describes his long absence in almost comic understatement as if it were a brief detour with an incidental delay. On another level of reading—that of communication from writer to reader as opposed to that of Jacob to Esau—Jacob is the quintessential latecomer (ואחר), the one who comes second from the womb, and sneaks from behind. This is how he sees himself and this is how Esau will remember him.

He later instructs the messengers who are to carry his offerings to Esau to "pass *before* me (לפני)" and to respond to Esau when he asks you "... who are these *before* you (לפניך)?" They are then instructed to tell Esau that

---

and 464. Kass nonetheless prefers other readings of the wrestling at Jabok than the "bifurcation" interpretation and he therefore uses the parallel in other ways.

Jacob is *behind us* (אחרינו). Subsequently, those who are walking *behind* (אחרי) the flocks are told to say as well that "Jacob your servant is *behind* us (אחרינו)" . . . "for he said [to himself] I will appease *his face* (פניו) with the gift that goes *in front* of me (לפני), and *after* (אחרי) this I will see *his face* (פניו), perhaps he will bear *my face* (פני).[7] The offering then passed before his [Esau's] *face* (פניו). . . ."

In a short space, the word אחר has appeared five times and the word פני an additional seven times. We readers are being prepared for the next scene where Jacob is struck *from behind* by the night time attacker and forced to wrestle *face to face* at a place that is then named by Jacob, Peniel (פניאל) (face of God, or facing God) and Penuel (פנואל) because he has finally seen the Lord *face to face* (פנים אל פנים) and has been redeemed. His name is then changed from Jacob (*behind, latecomer,* or he who *circumvents*) to Yisrael, which bears the connotations of *struggler, straight on* or *directed*,[8] as well as *one who confronts*. Again, the programmatically repeated words provide the reader with a vocabulary with which to decode the following scene. It is not simply that the latecomer who comes from behind will confront his nemesis face to face; more profoundly, the mode of *Jacobness* will undergo an "about face" in order to confront and engage that which had been previously deflected and evaded.

In Genesis 32:23, Jacob arises in the middle of the night, takes his wives, concubines, and eleven children and crosses the Jabok crossing. He crosses the river by that name and "transports all that is his." On the surface it seems that Jacob has crossed the Jabok together with his family and is now

---

[7] I have translated literally here in order to highlight the repetition of the Hebrew phrasing, though the idiomatic meaning of "bear my face" is clearly, "he will look graciously upon me."

[8] This connotation clearly relies on an identification of the letter *"sin"* in *Yisrael* with the letter *"shin"* in the word *"yashar."* This interchange of sin and shin and the connotation are certainly reinforced by the words in Isaiah 40:4, "the crooked shall be made straight" "והיה העקב למישור". There too, there is certainly a play on Jacob (the crooked) becoming *yashar* (straight).

on the other side, but we find him in the next verse alone, seemingly back on the far side of the river crossing.[9]

Several commentaries have sought explanation for Jacob being on the "wrong" side of the river. It would seem reasonable, in light of the overall context, that while this logistic anomaly is indicative of Jacob's ambivalence, it is primarily an underscoring of the central theme of the struggle at Jabok. In order to move forward, Jacob must first go back. There is indeed, as Rashi has suggested, *forgotten baggage*[10] on the other side, and before he can evolve, before he can become Yisrael, and before he can confront Esau, he must return to the source of his fears and repressions. Geography here is symbolic ground or psychological territory.

Yet another indication of the psychological nature of the topography is the idea of a *crossing* or *transition*. Moreover, the name of the river is *Jabok* (יבק), an approximate inversion of the name *Jacob* (יעקב). In the psychological territory marked off, Jacob will meet Jabok, that is to say, he will be turned inside out. That which was *behind him,* will come at him *face to face*, his past will meet him at the crossroads with his evolving future, and his very identity (the meaning of his name), will be reversed.

---

[9] This is the case for the readings of Rashi, his grandson Rashbam (Rabbi Samuel ben Meir), *The JPS Torah Commentary on Genesis* (N. Sarna, Excursus 24), and many other interpreters. Rashbam is most attentive to this paradox and describes Jacob as actually contemplating fleeing in the other direction due to his insurmountable fear of confrontation with Esau. This reading will receive support from the numerous parallels in language and content between this story and the flight of Jacob from Laban in the previous chapter. We will pursue those parallels in the coming pages. The text is not explicit as to the location of the struggle with the mysterious divine character, and it could indeed have taken place on either side of the river. A plain reading of context, however, would seem to support the reading of Rashi and Rashbam, and I will proceed accordingly.

[10] Rashi, echoing a prior midrash, has spoken of Jacob returning for "small vessels." I am suggesting that the forgotten baggage here is trauma, deception, his self image as an habitual avoider of conflict and as a man with little sense of entitlement. I am not imputing this allegorical understanding of "baggage" to Rashi or to his earlier sources, though it is possible they have something symbolic in mind when speaking of "small vessels."

Being turned inside out will be accomplished by a painful confrontation fraught with existential danger, as that which was buried will surface and the disconnections of a dis-integrated, bifurcated self will struggle for wholeness.

CHAPTER SEVEN

I AM JACOB

Genesis 32:25–33

25) And Jacob remained alone and a man wrestled with him until the rise of dawn.

26) And as he saw that he could not prevail against him, he wrenched Jacob's hip at the socket, so that the socket of his hip was strained as he wrestled with him.[1]

27) And he said, "Let me go, for the dawn is rising." But he said, "I will not let you go, unless you bless me."

28) And he said to him, "What is your name?" and he said, "Jacob."

29) And he said, "Your name shall no longer be called Jacob, but Yisrael, for you have confronted/competed [Hebrew *sarita* similar to root of *Yisrael*] with the divine and with the human and have prevailed [been able]."

30) And Jacob asked saying, "Please tell me your name," [Hebrew: **Hagida na she-mekha**], and he said, "why indeed ask my name?"

---

[1] In this verse I have adopted the NJPS translation.

And he blessed him there.

31) And Jacob named the place Peniel, because "I saw the Lord face to face (*panim el panim*), but my life was saved."

32) And the sun shone upon him as he passed Penuel, and he was limping on [favoring] his hip.

33) And thus the children of Israel shall not eat the sinew of the thigh [Hebrew: **Gid ha-na-she**] that is on the socket of the hip, to this very day, because he wrenched Jacob's hip socket at the sinew of the thigh.

(כה) וַיִּוָּתֵר יַעֲקֹב לְבַדּוֹ וַיֵּאָבֵק אִישׁ עִמּוֹ עַד עֲלוֹת הַשָּׁחַר:

(כו) וַיַּרְא כִּי לֹא יָכֹל לוֹ וַיִּגַּע בְּכַף יְרֵכוֹ וַתֵּקַע כַּף יֶרֶךְ יַעֲקֹב בְּהֵאָבְקוֹ עִמּוֹ:

(כז) וַיֹּאמֶר שַׁלְּחֵנִי כִּי עָלָה הַשָּׁחַר וַיֹּאמֶר לֹא אֲשַׁלֵּחֲךָ כִּי אִם בֵּרַכְתָּנִי:

(כח) וַיֹּאמֶר אֵלָיו מַה שְּׁמֶךָ וַיֹּאמֶר יַעֲקֹב:

(כט) וַיֹּאמֶר לֹא יַעֲקֹב יֵאָמֵר עוֹד שִׁמְךָ כִּי אִם יִשְׂרָאֵל כִּי שָׂרִיתָ עִם אֱ-לֹהִים וְעִם אֲנָשִׁים וַתּוּכָל:

(ל) וַיִּשְׁאַל יַעֲקֹב וַיֹּאמֶר הַגִּידָה נָּא שְׁמֶךָ וַיֹּאמֶר לָמָּה זֶּה תִּשְׁאַל לִשְׁמִי וַיְבָרֶךְ אֹתוֹ שָׁם:

(לא) וַיִּקְרָא יַעֲקֹב שֵׁם הַמָּקוֹם פְּנִיאֵל כִּי רָאִיתִי אֱ-לֹהִים פָּנִים אֶל פָּנִים וַתִּנָּצֵל נַפְשִׁי:

(לב) וַיִּזְרַח לוֹ הַשֶּׁמֶשׁ כַּאֲשֶׁר עָבַר אֶת פְּנוּאֵל וְהוּא צֹלֵעַ עַל יְרֵכוֹ:

(לג) עַל כֵּן לֹא יֹאכְלוּ בְנֵי יִשְׂרָאֵל אֶת גִּיד הַנָּשֶׁה אֲשֶׁר עַל כַּף הַיָּרֵךְ עַד הַיּוֹם הַזֶּה כִּי נָגַע בְּכַף יֶרֶךְ יַעֲקֹב בְּגִיד הַנָּשֶׁה

In contending with this passage, one is immediately struck by intense wordplay. Jacob יעקב meets a mysterious divine force of the night at Jabok

יבק and they proceed to wrestle ויאבק *vaje'abek*.[2] The action of striving or competing—*sarita,* results in the name *Yisrael;* the seeing of the Lord face to face, *panim el panim,* results in the naming of the place as *Peniel* and later *Penuel.* Less apparent at first glance, but an undeniable further instance of phonetic wordplay, is the Hebrew for "please tell me your name" (*hagid-a na-she mekha*) and the Hebrew for the twice repeated term, "the sinew of the thigh" (***gid ha-nashe.***[3]) This last instance of punning becomes all the more tantalizing as the term "*nashe*" as the location or description of a "*gid*" (sinew) is unique to this passage, and the meaning of the word is unclear. We will connect the meaning of the two phrases to their phonetic similarity in the following analysis.

The key to the mystery of this passage is clearly the identity of the stranger. At first, the narrative voice of the text (verse 25) simply calls him *ish*—a man. However, Jacob refers to him as (the) Lord (verse 31). In verse 29, the stranger may be referring to himself as both divine and as human when he says to Jacob, "you have striven (competed) with divine and with human." In other words, instead of seeing this verse as a reference to separate struggles with divine forces and human adversaries in separate unidentified episodes, it is likely—given the two variant descriptions surrounding this verse—that the stranger is at once identifying himself as both divine and human.

There is a divine presence that has hovered over Jacob since his dream at Beth-El (Gen. 28:13). There too, there were angels and a bridge connecting the divine and the human in the form of a ladder connecting heaven and earth. For Jacob's disconnected, *non-integrated* world, the innermost need is to create connections, to become whole. In fact, immediately following the successful confrontation and reunion with Esau, enabled by

---

[2] The term for wrestling here is a derivative of the Hebrew noun אבק *abak*—meaning dust. Thus, the connotation is of a struggle wherein dust is kicked up. Again, there is close phonetic mimicry between **abak, Jabok,** and **Jacob.**

[3] My thanks to former students Sara Wise Prager and Ilana Goldstein Saks who first pointed this out to me more than a decade ago.

the previous night's struggle, the verse describes Jacob arriving *shalem*— "whole"— at the city of Shechem (Gen. 33:18). Even if one understands *Shalem* here as a city named Salem, the meaning of the name has clear symbolic value, particularly given the prior repeated description of Jacob as bifurcated.[4]

As we shall see, this *night-time* being who combines heaven and earth, and has the power to bless Jacob thereby making him whole, functions in the story at least on one level as the mirror of Jacob's own *dark* side, of his repressed moral self-judgement. Simultaneously the stranger functions as the divine image within Jacob that bids him to become autonomous. The divine presence not only hovers above Jacob; it flutters within him. If Jacob can be whole, it is by struggling with the human and the divine within himself (verse 29). However, if he fails to confront his alter-ego face to face, if he continues life in the modus operandi of circumvention, he will be forever Jacob, never Yisrael. In this remarkable and cryptic passage of wordplay and symbolic namings, words metamorphose and with them our hero. Let us examine the process:

A man wrestles with Jacob at Jabok. The turning inside out of these words reflects the turning and tossing of the wrestling (*abek*). On another level, it will reflect the externalization of Jacob's long overdue internal struggle. Turning inside out will indeed be the turning of *inside* into *outside*. Dawn approaches and with it the night's struggle between interiority and its resistances moves dangerously toward illumination. At daybreak there is stalemate, no victor, no progress. Here a painful injury is incurred. Jacob, the "sneak from behind," is struck from behind; there is a sprain or minor dislocation. Jacob is the injured party, yet it is the night-time creature that begs release, an apparent inconsistency in the logic of the story (that is, unless one understands the struggle as an internal one.) It is the attacking man/angel that tells Jacob, "send me away for the dawn is rising."

---

[4] See the textual indications of this in our analysis above in chapter 6.

Why is this nocturnal force so afraid of daylight? What is it that needs at all costs to protect itself against *enlightenment?* Night-time must protect itself; that which has been repressed and relegated to the dark of the unconscious cannot risk the trauma of disclosure. The carefully constructed persona with all its narrow escapes and masquerades still has the advantage of remaining intact and of functioning, even if the cost is a bifurcated *self* of *two camps*, a conscious and a subconscious without ladders or angels to connect them.

Thus, we are prepared for yet another escape, yet another circumvention, still another retreat into darkness and repressed self-awareness. Jacob's other half begs for release before daylight, and everything points to the relief of separation for both adversaries. But here the story and our hero surprise us.

Though Jacob has been accosted and injured, *he* is now the one who refuses to let go, and he tells us why. The blessing! "I will not let you go unless you *bless* me," (32:27). Jacob has the chance to let his resistances remain in place, to send away the repressed identity of Jacob—the heel-grabber, the taker of birthrights and blessings, the Jacob of "I am Esau, your first-born." But if he does so now, he will remain **unentitled** at the deepest levels of identity and moral integrity. Most urgently, he will be incapable of facing Esau the next morning. It is clear beyond doubt why it is specifically at this crossing, at Jabok, and at this moment in time, that Jacob will muster the courage to face his internal demons. It is now or never, and Jacob will not, cannot, circumvent any longer. He refuses the request for release and in effect, says:

> "I will not let go, I will wrestle to the end, for I must gain belated entitlement to the *blessing.*"

At this point, the mysterious being that has served until now as both threatening adversary and mirror of self, switches gears and assumes a con-

126

ciliatory posture. Still playing the role of "mirror of self," this therapeutic man/angel now guides the injured party in need of blessing or wholeness by asking just the right question at precisely the right moment. In doing so, he is again simply mirroring the words he has heard and presenting their underlying meaning. Having already assumed the position of "mirror," he is uniquely suited to fill this role.

Jacob has asked for a blessing, and we—together with this mysterious figure who mirrors Jacob's inner demons—can hardly refrain from remarking: "A blessing? Very interesting choice of words!" With exquisite intuition and timing, this vehicle of psychoanalytic reflection then leads Jacob back to the scene where, in order to receive the blessing, Jacob was first asked by the suspicious Isaac, "Who are you, my son?" At that moment, Jacob had prevaricated, responding, "I am Esau your firstborn," in order to achieve the result of possessing the birthright and the blessing. Paradoxically and ironically, that became the critical moment not of *possessing* but of being *possessed*, of becoming a man no longer in control of his own destiny and no longer sure of his entitlement to even the most basic aspects of self-identity.[5] Thus, the mirror/adversary knew to return precisely to this moment when he asks Jacob the one deceptively simple but existentially pivotal question, "What is your name?"

Repetition—until now in the Jacob narratives—had taken the form of a compulsive return to the point of repressed trauma—as the troubled unconscious was continually striving toward resolution. It is now deployed as an artificially manipulated repetition scene, designed for therapeutic effect.[6]

This time, in order to receive the blessing, Jacob must again answer the same question that the blind Isaac had asked decades earlier. Who are you?

---

[5] See the definition of the neurotic personality in David Shapiro's seminal book, *Psychotherapy of Neurotic Character* (USA: Basic Books, 1999), especially pages 3–13. I am grateful to Henri Zukier for his helpful formulation that inability to *possess* and being *possessed* are intimately related in the Jacob narratives.

[6] See my Introduction, pages 33–35.

What is your name? This time Jacob utters the words, "I am Jacob," a symbolic rectification and reversal of his previous denial of self-identification. Jacob has replayed the moment that had encapsulated the relinquishing of his moral autonomy. Immediately, the adversary turned therapist—the one capable of bestowing blessings and restoring wholeness, primarily by listening well and by asking the right questions—responds by saying: "Your name shall no longer be called Jacob but rather Yisrael, for you have struggled/confronted with the divine and the human. . . ."

Paradoxically—but surprisingly in consonance with various theories of the development of identity—only when fully acknowledging and internalizing one's past can one's identity evolve or proceed to the next stage of development. Jacob cannot become Yisrael until he can say, "I am Jacob." That this is the relationship between verses 28 and 29—going back in order to go forward—is indicated as well by the backward-forward nature of the geography of the river crossings as psychological turf. It is also borne out, as we shall see, by a look at Genesis chapter 35, verses 9 and 10.

The scene at Jabok where the man/angel changes the name Jacob to Yisrael is both echoed and confirmed in Genesis chapter thirty-five, where God himself appears to Jacob upon his long awaited return to Beth-El and his fulfillment of the vow. God blesses Jacob and says to him: "**Your name is Jacob**, you shall no longer be called Jacob, but rather Yisrael shall be your name, and he called his name Yisrael" (35:10).

The odd but clearly purposeful repetition at the beginning of this verse—"**your name is Jacob**"—before continuing to say that "you shall no longer be called Jacob," again highlights the need for owning one's past in order to move toward the future.[7] Moreover, this seems to confirm that Jacob's uttering the words "**I am Jacob**" was indeed the crucial *sine qua non* for his change of name in the previous scene of name change in chapter 32.

---

[7] I am grateful to my former student Yael Brenner for first calling this to my attention.

It is of further significance that this confirmation by God at Beth-El—of the prior name change at Jabok—immediately follows the death and burial of Devorah, Rebecca's nurse maid (Gen. 35:8). This verse is unusual in two ways: Devorah is mentioned by name only in this verse.[8] It is also anomalous in the entire Bible to introduce a character only at death. It would seem that burying this ancient character (the adult Jacob's mother's nursemaid), signifies yet another prerequisite to the metamorphosis of Jacob to Yisrael. This, after all, is Jacob, perhaps only now belatedly "weaned" from his mother Rebecca's influence. This is Jacob, who inappropriately relinquished his autonomy to a mother who dressed her adult son in another's clothing and told him, "listen to my voice. . . your curse shall be upon me." Now, at this juncture, upon Jacob's return to Beth-El and just prior to the moment of the divine reconfirmation of his new identity, he must divest himself of the last vestigial ties to that inappropriate dependence. This is expressed symbolically in the burial of a mythic woman who has silently accompanied Rebecca and then Jacob through their lives, and whose role, despite her years, is still described as one who nourishes from the breast. Implied is that even as Jacob fled the house of Rebecca, the *breast-feeding of Rebecca* accompanied him throughout his years in Laban's house until his return to Beth-El.

Returning to the critical moment at the Jabok crossing, the change of name to Yisrael is explained in the verse (32:29) as "*sarita*—you have struggled [Yisra-el from the same word *s-r-h*], with divine beings and with men, ותוכל—*vatukhal*—and you have **prevailed**." The translation of the last word of this pronouncement as "*you have prevailed*," by virtually all translators, should be called into question. The sense of *prevailed* is assumed because of this verse's connection to the earlier verse (32:26) where the mysterious adversary sees that he cannot *prevail* against Jacob and then

---

[8] Rebecca's nursemaid was previously introduced in Gen. 24:59, but without being named.

resorts to smiting him below the belt, on the socket of his thigh.[9]

However, in verse 29, the Hebrew ends with the word *vatukhal* and does not, as in the previous verse, add the word **להם** or another word with the preposition "**ל**" that would make the meaning *prevailed* as opposed to this verb root's usual meaning—*to become able* or *empowered*. Though the connection between verses 26 and 29 would certainly justify translating the word in verse 29 as "you have *prevailed*," there is more than justification for adhering to the standard meaning of *tukhal* as "enabled." To presume the addition of a missing preposition, as most translators do, effectively and unfortunately eliminates the alternative reading of "*tukhal*" as "to become able."[10]

In short, there is strong linguistic and contextual support for an unconventional understanding of the outcome of the struggle and the subsequent blessing as ***empowerment***. One might indeed translate or interpret the end of verse 29: "you have struggled with that which is divine and that

---

[9] In that verse, we find the same verb root—*yakhol* **יכל**—that appears in our verse in the form *tukhal* **תוכל**. Indeed, the verb *yakhol* almost always understood as "to be able," does consistently take on the meaning of "*prevail*" when the next word is preceded by the prepositional prefix *le-*, literally "*to*" or here, *against*). Thus, the translation *prevail* in verse 26 (where the phrase is **יכל לו** *yakhol lo*) is accurate. Occasionally, but rarely, the word *yakhol* does appear without a subsequent '*l*,' yet clearly with the meaning *to prevail*. See Gen. 30:8 and I Samuel 26:25.

[10] It is entirely in keeping with the subtle use of purposeful asymmetry in biblical literary style to juxtapose two verses with similar language while cutting one verse short in order to create comparison and contrast simultaneously. Here, the use of '*yakhol l*' in one verse to mean **prevail** and *yakhol* by itself *(vatukhal)* to mean **enabled**, creates artful understatement. Similarly, toward the beginning of the strife between Joseph and his brothers, in Gen. 37:4, the text states that the brothers "could not speak to him in peace"—**ולא יכלו דברו לשלם**. In subtle contrast, toward the end of Genesis with a tentative rapprochement between the brothers, the verse (Gen. 45:15) records, "and afterward [after Joseph reveals himself to them and speaks to them in a conciliatory tone] his brothers spoke to him," **דברו אחיו אתו**. It is poignant and telling at the same time that they finally speak to Joseph, but not yet "in peace." Understatement is conveyed through asymmetry; resolution of outward strife or internal struggle is seldom swift and complete, but more often incremental and partial.

which is human and you are enabled."

The distinction between victory and empowerment is of critical importance. It is difficult to support a reading of "victory," as the struggle seems very clearly to continue, just as the change of name is not final and irrevocable. Jacob continues to be called Jacob as well as Yisrael even after the divine confirmation of the name change in chapter 35. Moreover, in subsequent episodes in Jacob's life, he does seem to behave in a decidedly "Jacobly" manner. This understanding of the change of name as an evolving identity that does not discard the previous name or identity is essential to a nuanced psychological understanding of the transition at Jabok.

This idea may be subtly indicated in an earlier verse that has always been troubling because of its unusual content and phrasing. After Jacob awakens from the dream of the "ladder" to the heavens and just before he utters his vow, he names the place of his epiphany Beth-El (house of God). But a very odd parenthetic post script is then tacked to the end of that verse (Gen. 28:19):

> "He called the name of that place Beth-El, however, Luz was the name of the city previously."

What is the significance of the rather terse text supplying us with rare historical geographical information, and providing it after the new naming as if to emphasize that *the name wasn't always what it has become and there is importance in preserving the old name.* The significance may lie in the effect of foreshadowing that this **renamed** location (Luz—Beth-El) will be the site of Jacob's own **renaming** in chapter 35 upon his return from Laban's house. In that renaming, as well, the prior name and identity will not only be preserved but will be reaffirmed as indispensable for the further evolution of identity.[11]

---

[11] This emphasis on the renaming of Beit-El crops up again in Judges 1:22–26. There is one additional instance in the Hebrew Bible of the phrase, clearly in

Moreover, the prior name of this town, *Luz*, oddly appears in the next chapter as the name of a tree from which Jacob fashions a rod to be used in the secret manipulation of the speckled, spotted and striped features of Laban's flocks. "Then Jacob took a rod from fresh poplar, almond (*Luz*), and plane (*Armon*). . ." (Gen. 31:37). This rod—used to manipulate Laban's wealth and transfer it to Jacob—is omitted in Jacob's retelling (in Gen. 31:4–12) to his wives of the "miraculous" divine intervention on his behalf. There, the maneuvers that appear in chapter 30 as Jacob's ingenuity and cunning, appear as a divinely revealed promise of recompense for Laban's years as an exploitative employer. The idea is that—as a name change in which the former identity must be recognized—*Luz* foreshadows and reflects *Jacob* in much the same way as *Beth-El* represents *Yisra-el;* one might find further support in the curious fact that the root *Luz* in biblical Hebrew seems to mean "deviate" or "devious" much like the meanings of the root עקב of *Jacob*.[12]

---

imitation of the verse in Genesis 28. In Judges 18:29, at the tail end of the story of an unidentified Levite who served as a priest to the tribe of Dan in pagan worship, the Dan tribe settles in Lebanon, builds a city and names it Dan after their ancestor. After naming the city, the end of the verse informs us that "**Layish was the name of the city previously.**" The next verse informs us after two full chapters concerning the unidentified Levite, that his name was Yehonathan the son of Gershom the son of Menashe. In the masoretic text, the word *Menashe* מנשה is written with the letter "n"—"נ" extended above the line, the result—a reading of the name of the father of Gershom as Moshe and not Menashe. Recall that Moshe, a Levite, was indeed the father of Gershom. Midrashic sources suggest that the author or scribe of this book has chosen to thinly veil the identity of Moses (Moshe) in order to spare him from the ignominy of having idol worshipping offspring. If this is indeed the case, we would have an idiosyncratically precise parallel to the verse of the previously named "Luz." Here too, the renaming of a city is connected to the renaming of a person. And here too, the new name of the person (Menashe, like Yisrael), does not completely obscure or replace the original name (Moshe or Jacob). Thus, Beth-El is identified as "still Luz" and Dan is "still Layish." (Cleverly, the name "Moshe" is shielded from ready identification or *caused to be forgotten* by becoming "Menashe" which means to *cause to be forgotten*.)

[12] See Proverbs 4:21 and 4:24. A further indication that wordplay is at work here in describing Jacob's "devious" fashioning of the rod of *Luz* might be the name of

132

Another support for reading *tukhal* as empowerment and not as victory—and for seeing the prior identity as still exerting its inertia—comes from the various episodes that follow. In the coming chapters, Jacob continues to reflect in his life choices the character of *Jacobness*—denial and avoidance, alongside that of *sarita-Yisrael*—straightforward confrontation with self and with circumstance.[13] The ancient Midrash literature emphasized this very point when it highlights the fact that once Abram's name is changed to Abraham, he is never again called Abram, and once Sarai becomes Sarah, she is never again referred to as Sarai. Yet, Jacob is continually referred to as Jacob even after the divine conferral of his new name—Yisrael.[14]

At most, one gets a sense of empowerment, not of victorious metamorphosis as the most apt epitaph or title for this pivotal scene of wrestling and name change. Through a painful confrontation with his own repressed identity, a confrontation that carries with it lasting injury or vulnerability, Jacob has become enabled—"*vatukhal.*"

Both the "disabling" nature of the therapeutic breakthrough and the temporary nature of the newly gained self-awareness are underscored in David Shapiro's description of the course of therapeutic change. He could have been speaking of Jacob when he wrote:

"We introduce a patient to himself. . . We see a change in him; he

---

another tree used in the same description of the rod—"*armon.*" In this word as well, the root ערם is used elsewhere to mean "devious," e.g., Genesis 3:1.

[13] Note, particularly, Jacob's parting exchange with Esau on the morrow, where Esau offers joint travel under his protection and Jacob declines, claiming that he will catch up to Esau later, at Mt. Se'ir. The claim appears to be disingenuous as Jacob never goes there.

The name *Se'ir* as "goat" (the goats of the deception scene?) as well as meaning "hairy"—Jacob's prior description of Esau (Gen. 27:11)—provides further indication of geography as psychological territory and may explain why Jacob does not want to "go there." My thanks to Tzvi Mauer for this latter suggestion.

[14] See *Bereishit Rabba* 78:5.

feels a change in himself. . . Yet a week or two later he may talk about the same thing in. . . much the same way he did originally, as if the new awareness has left him. Why should the same territory have to be won again and again? . . . Self awareness, once achieved, we have thought, deprives those restrictive dynamics [i.e., the sense of being possessed rather than possessing, the sense of a constricted autonomy—S.K.] of their automatic engagement and their force.... When we intervene and articulate what the patient cannot spontaneously articulate—when we act in that way to enlarge his self-awareness—we penetrate the otherwise reflexively triggered limits of the restrictive system, and in doing so we—theoretically—disable it. And indeed it seems we do, momentarily. Yet not a week later. . . ."[15]

Furthermore, Bruno Bettelheim has observed that many mistakenly view psychoanalysis as having the purpose of making life easy, or of achieving some kind of victory over the contentious forces within us. "But this is not what its founder intended. Psychoanalysis was created to **enable** man to accept the problematic nature of life without being defeated by it, or giving in to escapism. Freud's prescription is that only by **struggling** [emphasis mine—S.K.] against what seem like overwhelming odds can man succeed in wringing meaning out of existence."[16]

Both Shapiro and Bettelheim warn practitioners as well as patients that the successful outcome of analysis will never be outright victory, but rather an enhanced and more autonomous struggle. That this is one of the central themes of the Genesis narratives should also be clear from the parallel message given to Cain just before his murder of Abel (Gen. 4:7), ". . . sin crouches at the door and to you shall be its desire, but you

[15] David Shapiro, *Psychotherapy of Neurotic Character,* 194.
[16] Bruno Bettelheim, *The Uses of Enchantment* (NY: Vintage Books, 1977) 8.

can rule over it."[17] Mortals will continually struggle with their own conflicting desires and emotions, and we are not promised victory, only the empowerment for struggle.

What is the key to Jacob's advance toward *"vatukhal,"* toward enabling? The answer may lie in what is perhaps the most difficult phrase in the entire episode at Jabok, the anomalous phrase, *"gid ha-nashe,"* (Gen. 32:33). "And thus the children of Israel shall not eat the sinew of the thigh [Hebrew transliteration: *gid ha-na-she*] that is on the socket of the hip, to this very day, because he wrenched Jacob's hip socket at the sinew of the thigh."

Clearly referring to a part of the human anatomy, this phrase has been translated variously as "sinew on the socket of the thigh," as "the sciatic nerve," and as "the thigh muscle." Clearly, as there is a lasting prohibition for the children of Israel not to eat from this part of an animal's anatomy, the **gid ha-nashe**, has symbolic meaning beyond its anatomic specificity. Given the pervasive use of wordplay throughout this episode, it is reasonable that the key to the symbolism of the phrase will be its phonetic similarity to the phrase three verses earlier, *hagida na shemecha*—"pray, **tell** me your name." In that phrase, the word "ha**gid**" means *to tell* rather than *gid*, as *sinew*. Again, the possibility of syllepsis as an intertextual indicator must be explored.

This injury, this striking or dislocating of the *gid (sinew),* on the one hand causes Jacob to walk away limping and vulnerable, but on the other hand seems to make him even more *able* or *empowered* in his struggle. It seems, furthermore, that through phonetic wordplay, this enabling injury is to be associated with **hagid**—with *"telling."*[18] Moreover, it seems to involve the telling of names, the significance of which we have already begun to explore. In fact, as we have suggested, Jacob has symbolically confronted

---

[17] See the wonderful passage on the proper way to translate this verse in John Steinbeck's *East of Eden* (NY: Penguin, 1981) 348–9.

[18] We are immediately reminded of Freud's early reference to his partner Breuer's patient Anna O. —who referred to the latter's treatment of her as "the talking cure."

his past precisely in the act of the ***telling of his own name.***

But what is the symbolic meaning of identifying this ***gid*** *sinew* or *telling* as the ***gid*** of the ***nashe?*** Here, various commentaries have attempted to connect this unique word with nouns or verb roots that are similar.[19] One of the more intriguing suggestions in explaining this term appears in Rashi's commentary. He connects the use of *nashe* with verse 51 in Genesis chapter forty-one, where the verb appears with the meaning, *to remove* or *to cause to forget*. While Rashi concludes that it is therefore called *nashe* because the sinew has been *moved or dislocated* from its place, it would be worthwhile to entertain a more powerful connection with the appearance of the root *nashe* in chapter 41. The implication then of the appearance of the anomalous term *gid hanashe* here in Chapter 32 would be to translate the *"dislocated sinew"* alternatively as the *"telling of the forgotten."*

In order to fully interpret the superimposition onto our text of the term *"nashe"* from chapter 41, we must take a closer look at the word's use in the later story that served as Rashi's lexical reference: In Genesis Chapter 41, Joseph has risen from his sale into slavery at the hands of his brothers—and from his imprisonment on false charges of sexual harassment—to the highest position in the Egyptian Pharaoh's government. He has made a success of his ability to interpret dreams with God's help and has now married an Egyptian woman. He names the older of the two sons born to him, *"Menashe*—מנשה—for God has ***caused me to forget (nashani)***— נשני—all my tribulations and all my father's house." That which Joseph thanks God for *causing him to forget* is the trauma of his father's house—his being thrown into a pit and sold into slavery by his brothers.

---

[19] One such possibility that is implied but not explicitly suggested by the Midrash cited above (pages 90–91) is that the word *nashe* here is connected to the same root that is used thirteen times in the Hebrew Bible to mean "collection of a debt." This injury, then, could be seen as the *payback* for Jacob's debt to Esau or for the as yet unpaid vow to God at Beth-El. This interpretation need not replace the one I will adopt in the coming section; on the contrary, it seems to augment and support the alternative meaning of *nashe* as to *remove* or *cause to forget*.

If one were to suggest the most appropriate synonym for *to cause to forget,* it would certainly be *to repress,* and herein lies the most perfect paradox. Joseph is keen on starting a new life, and leaving behind the pit and his sale into slavery. He is so preoccupied with his effort to start anew and to put the past behind him that on the occasion of beginning his life as an Egyptian with a new wife and son, he names the child *Menashe,* or "forget my father's house."

The biblical text seems exquisitely aware of the irony it has called forth. It is the ancient Hebrew equivalent of a newly successful Yiddish speaking immigrant in America naming his son *Repressele.* By naming his firstborn "forget my father's house," he has ensured that no such thing can ever occur. But this is, of course, the very nature of all repression; by relegating one's traumatic past to the subconscious, it is not only hidden from consciousness, it is also preserved. Joseph cannot really escape the consequences of his own behavior, or of that of his brothers, until he confronts the past rather than avoiding or resisting it.

Returning to Jacob and the sinew of the thigh—*(gid hanashe),* it may now be proposed that the *telling (**gid**)* is that of the **nashe** or *dislocated* in the sense of the telling of the repressed. This is the way the term **nashe** is used in the Joseph story where the rare word appears in a form closest to its lexical form in our passage.[20] Jacob, like Joseph, cannot escape the consequences of his own dealings and "misdealings" with his brother or father until he confronts the past—retelling it—rather than avoiding or resisting it.

---

[20] In fact, one is tempted to see this parallel between the *repression of father's house* in both the Jacob and Joseph stories as yet another sophisticated instance of the "measure for measure" literary construct that typifies and unites the respective narratives of father and son. As Jacob has ruptured the father-son relationship in deceiving his own father, Jacob's son is removed from his father through deceit and mistakenly looks back at his own father as part of a former life that must be forgotten. See the novel interpretation of the Joseph story in Yoel Bin-Nun's essay in *"Megadim"* vol. 1 (Alon Shevut, Herzog College, 1986) 20–31.

On the surface level of reading and storyline, the "enabling" *(vatukhal)* injury is that of the dislocated sinew. But as indicated by context, by intertextual reference, and by sophisticated phonetic wordplay, it is also a threatening and simultaneously cathartic injury that accompanies a struggle and confrontation with self. And all of this involves at its core— the *gid hanashe* as the *telling of the repressed.*

Even in a text as loaded with phonetic wordplay as this, we search for further contextual support for the two tiered reading of this biblical passage based on wordplay—i.e., *gid* as *to tell,* in addition to *sinew,* and *nashe* as *repressed* or *removed from consciousness,* in addition to *dislocated.* To demonstrate the additional literary grounding for this reading, we return to the confrontation with Laban in chapter thirty-one of Genesis, which will, in turn, heighten our awareness of the extensive and intensive parallel between that scene and Jacob's confrontation with the mysterious wrestler of chapter thirty-two.

In chapter thirty-one, the verb *ganov,* גנב—*"to steal"*—appears eight times between 31:19 and 31:39, and the nearly synonymous *gazol* appears once. There are two other key words that appear in strategic relation to stealing. As we have noted, the word *barach,* ברח—"to flee"—appears four times in verses 31:20 through 31:27, and forms of the verb *higgid*—*"to tell"* appear three times in the same short interval. In both verse twenty and in verse twenty-seven, the three key words are used in tight sequence:

> Verse 20) "And Jacob **stole** (ויגנב) the heart of Laban the Aramean by not **telling** (הגיד) him that he was **fleeing** (ברח).

> Verse 27) "Why have you concealed your **fleeing** (לברח); you have **stolen** (ותגנב) me and have not **told** (הגדת) me...."

Until the crossing at Jabok, Jacob's modus operandi is insistent avoidance of confrontation; *fleeing* or evasion, *stealing* away, and *not telling,* are his trademarks. As we have demonstrated, the evasion, repression, and failures *to tell* are not simply with others, but even more significantly they typify the short-circuited communication between Jacob's own conscious and unconscious. It is this latter disconnection that has been most debilitating to Jacob, and must be healed at the cost of injury in order to *enable* further development of identity signified by name change. In the scene where **Jacob** is turned inside out (that of the **Jabok** crossing), he must tell (ha**gid**) the repressed trickery of the **g'di** (goat) that posed as venison and whose skin impersonated Esau's hairy arms. The injury of the **gid** (sinew) compensates for the **g'di**, just as the next day with Esau, the **mincha** (offering) offered Esau will substitute for the **machane** (encampment)[21] that Jacob needs to protect, and the **berakha**—blessing (but in context: the gift), offered Esau—will belatedly validate the **bekhora** (birthright) that had been taken.[22]

All of Jacob's previous episodes of deception, of his father, his brother, of Laban, all of his acts of **stealing away**, of **not telling**, of **evasion** and escape, are now emblematically reenacted and confronted. Above all, the *g'di*—the goat of deception—finds rehabilitation in the form of the sinew, the *gid—the telling*.

Aside from the important identification of the key words that become key themes—**to steal, to flee, to fail to tell**, the confrontation with Laban (chapter 31) prepares both Jacob and the reader in additional ways for the confrontation at Jabok (chapter 32): In both chapters, Jacob is accosted or overtaken at a river crossing. In both stories there is initial conflict and struggle—with the threatened Jacob ultimately receiving the blessing of his adversary. In recognition of the reconciliation of the adversaries in both stories, the sites of the struggles receive special names. But the parallel of chapter 31 to chapter 32 goes beyond the foreshadowing of

---

[21] The words מחנה *machane* and מנחה *mincha* are used repeatedly as key words in chapters 32 and 33.

[22] Gen. 33:11.

storyline, as there is highly idiosyncratic parallel language in describing the two encounters:

Chapter 31: Jacob and Laban	Chapter 32: Jacob and the stranger
ויגנב יעקב...על בלי **הגיד** לו כי ברח הוא... **ויגד** ללבן כי ברח יעקב... למה נחבאת לברח...ולא **הגדת** לי and Jacob stole the heart of Laban by **not telling (higid)** him that he was about to *flee*. . . and it was **told (yugad)** to Laban. . . that Jacob had *fled*. . . why have you secretly *fled* by not **telling (higadeta)** me. . . 3 X hi**gid** in Gen. 31:20–27	**הגידה** נא שמך...לא יאכלו בני ישראל את **גיד** הנשה...כי נגע בכף ירך יעקב ...**בגיד** הנשה . . . please **tell (hagida)** your name. . . the children of Israel shall not eat of the **gid** ha-nashe. . . for he had touched the socket of the thigh of Jacob at the **gid** (sinew). 3 X **gid** in Gen. 32:30–33
ויעקב **תקע** את אהלו...ולבן **תקע** את אחיו... And Jacob *pitched* (**taka**) his tent. . . and Laban with his brothers *encamped* (**taka**) (31:25)	...**ותקע** כף ירך יעקב And Jacob's socket of his hip was *strained*. . . (va-**teka**) (31:26)
שלחני ואלכה למקומי... ריקם **שלחתני** (**shalkhani**). . . (**shilakhtani**) *send me free and I will go to my land*. . . you would have *sent me free empty handed* (30:25). . . (31:42)	**שלחני** כי עלה השחר ... ויאמר לא **אשלחך** (**shalkhani**. . . **ashalekhecha**) . . . *send me free* for the dawn is rising; and he said, ' I will not *send you free*. . . (32:27)
יגיע כפי **ראה** א-להים (**yegia capai ra'ah**) God *saw*... the *toil of my hands* (31:42)	**וירא** כי לא יכל לו **ויגע בכף** ירכו (**vayar [form of ra'ah] vayiga** b'**caph**) He *saw* that he could not prevail and he *touched the socket of his hip* (32:26)
ויאכלו שם And they *ate* there. . . (va**yochelu**) (31:46)	על כן לא **יאכלו** And therefore. . . shall not *eat* (**yochelu**) (32:33)
ויברך אתהם . . . . and he [Laban] *blessed* them. . . (**vayevarech**) (32:1)	**ויברך** אותו And he [the angelic stranger] *blessed* him. . . (**vayevarech**) (32:30)

140

The density and highly idiosyncratic use of similar language in the two confrontation scenes—particularly in the Hebrew of 31:42 and 32:26, where a rare combination of words appears almost identically in both with totally different meanings—strongly indicates that the prior scene parallels the later one. In fact, the thrice repeated use of the key word *hagid*—"*to tell*"—provides further confirmation that the three repetitions of the same phoneme (*gid*) in the next chapter—once as "to tell" and twice as "sinew"—are meant to serve as double entendre. The additional examples of wordplay or syllepsis, wherein identical words or phonemes carry differing meanings (**taka, yiga, caf**), also confirms the claim that ***gid ha-nashe*** (32:33) and *ha-**gid**-a na she-mekha* (32:30) are meant to associate the *sinew* with the *telling*.

Moreover, what is the evasion or falsehood that has been repressed *(nashe)* and now needs to be spoken *(hagid)*? Of course, it concerns Jacob's name *(shemekha)*. Jacob had "dislocated" his true identity when he assumed the false identity of "I am Esau." By telling his real name ("I am Jacob") in order to receive the blessing of his adversary, Jacob has finally become blessed. And on the level of literary "triple-entendre," we have now arrived at a profound identification of ***gid hanashe*** as both "dislocated sinew" and as "telling of the forgotten [repressed]," with its phonetic echo—*ha**gida na** shemekha*, "pray tell me your name."

The scene with Laban, as we have seen, replays the original deception scene, conforming to the pattern of the compulsive return of Jacob to the pivotal moment of fracture of identity and loss of autonomy. The unresolved must unconsciously be recreated in the hopes of being reworked. Jacob failed to tell his father the truth, he had caused his brother to hate him, and he was forced into fleeing. Similarly here, Laban —and the narrative voice of the text—accuse Jacob of stealing Laban's heart, the manipulation of the speckled and spotted sheep causes Jacob's brothers-in-law to hate him, and he is forced to flee.

But just as this parting scene with Laban echoes and resonates with the past, it also prepares us for the following scene with the wrestling angel. Reciprocally, the scene at Jabok replays and reworks the earlier scene with Laban.

Additionally, the scene at Jabok has transported Jacob to another level and the narrative to yet another genre of repetition. This time, as we have said, it takes the form of an artificially induced therapeutic recreation of the original scene that is necessary in order to regain identity and integrity, integration and wholeness. Just as the night wrestler mirrors Jacob's repressed identity, the situation of saying one's name in order to receive the blessing must mirror the moment that encapsulates his repressed forfeiture of moral autonomy.

Ironically, the devious and misguided attempt to gain entitlement sent Jacob into a deep-seated sense of lack of entitlement and into a repeated orbit of further evasions and circumventions. Conversely, at this point of reversal, the ultimate regaining of entitlement and integrity had to be achieved by confrontation with self, and (on the morrow), with Esau through acts of humility, magnanimity and vulnerability. Jacob, the empowered, walks away from Jabok limping (32:32), and proceeds to prostrate himself seven times while approaching Esau (33:3). Again, paradoxically, the limping Jacob is now described as "whole" (Gen. 33:18).

"And the sun shone upon him as he passed **Penuel** [literally: confronting the Lord], and he was limping on his thigh" (Gen. 32:32). Jacob's *enlightenment dawns* upon him through confronting the Lord, through a wrestling with self, with others and with God that is simultaneously an injury and an enabling *(vatukhal)* moment of evolving identity.

CHAPTER EIGHT

HUMAN AUTONOMY
VERSUS
COVENANTAL DESTINY

I have tried to take a fresh look at the very old and familiar story of Isaac, Rebecca, Jacob, and Esau.

In the Bible, it seems that one's redemption, one's wholeness, one's *berakha* (blessing), cannot come about by way of circumventions or by dubious moral behavior; the evolution of Jacob into *Yisrael* cannot bypass Jacob's being Jacob. It is precisely in the act of trying to accomplish the prophetic vision of "the older shall serve the younger" that Rebecca and Jacob falter and unwittingly send the divine plan into prolonged remission. It is exactly because Jacob has relinquished his autonomy and identity by saying "I am Esau" that he reverses the very Abrahamic blessing that he is trying to receive, symbolically fleeing from Canaan back to Haran. One cannot "strive with God"—the meaning of the name *Yisrael*—without first confronting others and self face to face. It is the mistaken notion that God's plan supersedes the autonomous, judicious exercise of one's divinely imbued moral sense that repeatedly gets our biblical heroes into trouble.

But how are the fragile but heroic biblical characters—with their fractured sense of wholeness—to balance the demands of self-mastery with their awareness of their role in the drama of a transcendent sovereign?

The recognition that divine plan and human moral accountability proceed along independent routes—that paradoxically merge only when each path maintains its integrity and coherence—comes late in the book of Genesis. In the Joseph stories, that echo the Jacob narratives of jealousy, inability to communicate, and near-fratricide, the brothers act cruelly and deceitfully in trying to frustrate Joseph's dreams. When the brothers finally appear in Joseph's court, the latter, in turn, deals cruelly and deceitfully with them in what would seem to be an attempt to fulfill his dreams (of the brothers bowing down to him). At the initial reconciliation of the brothers, Joseph tries to whitewash the sordid events of the past by attributing everything to divine providence:

> "I am Joseph your brother whom you sold into Egypt. Now do not be grieved, nor angry with yourselves... for God did send me here before you to preserve life.... It was **not** you who sent me here, but God...." (Gen. 45:5–8)

Ultimately, the whitewash is proven ineffective and the reconciliation revealed as hollow, as relationships, like individual identities, cannot evolve on the basis of evasions, repressions, or revisions of the past. There must be self-recognition and painful encounter with the other and with one's own accountability. Thus, when Jacob dies, the brothers once again fear the powerful Joseph's retribution (Gen. 50:15). This time Joseph understands that reconciliation requires a more credible recognition of the past. It seems he has also arrived at a more sophisticated teleological conception, in which flawed and misguided human endeavors interact with divine providence but often do not reflect it.

In the closing verses of Genesis, Joseph speaks again to his fearful brothers, saying: "Fear not, for am I in place of God?[1] But as for you, you thought evil against me, but God meant it for good..." (Gen. 50:19–20). This mode of rapprochement bears the potential for success; it is enabling. Though confrontational, it bears the stamp of sincerity and integrity and it avoids the perpetuation of conflict that is the fate of all circumvention and repression.

Both in terms of Joseph's own behavior ("am I in place of God?") and in terms of his brothers' culpability ("you thought evil"), Joseph has no longer justified human malevolence or treachery on the basis of its fortuitous co-incidence with the divine plan. Yet, at the same time, he understands the human predicament as intimately and mysteriously connected to God's providential direction. The two, human history and the divine plan, will meet, but it will not be man's task to determine or anticipate in which way or at what moment. The only path out of the thicket will be blazed by our pursuit of the autonomous realization of the divine image within us.

The biblical view has staked much on its belief in human autonomy and on the concept of covenantal destiny. Yet it does not do so from the perspective of an underestimation of the difficult, complex and heroic nature of the duality of the challenge. Because our repressions, resistances, and our carefully constructed false identities are so deeply and inextricably connected to our being who we are, it will require courage and tenacity to listen attentively to our souls, to build a bridge between voice and action—a ladder between one's internal heaven and earth. It is in the heroic moment

---

[1] One cannot but hear in these words an echo of the earlier exclamation of Joseph's father, Jacob (Genesis 30:2). In fact, these are the only two verses in the entire Hebrew Bible where this phrase appears. Jacob had used nearly identical language to respond to Rachel's demand for children: "**Am I in place of God** who withheld children from you?" Yet, one gets the sense that in Jacob's impulsive response to Rachel, these words express the shepherd's frustration with his own powerlessness. However, the powerful viceroy Joseph, apparently in control of his own destiny and that of countless others, is now using the same words to express his own mature humility—a belated but profound recognition regarding the limits of human manipulation in the context of cosmic divine planning.

of "I shall not set you free, for I need the blessing," and paradoxically in the recognition of one's own vulnerability (Jacob walked away limping) that one is *enabled*. With the painful but cathartic encounter with the self, comes the power to struggle. Jacob/Yisrael is "Everyman"—bisected, analyzed, integrated, and struggling to be blessed.

CHAPTER NINE

HUMILITY AND HUBRIS:
THE DONKEY AND THE BIRD

As in the previous chapters examining the episodes of Jacob's life, cul-minating in the scene at the Jabok crossing, this chapter will also examine stories in which the relationship between divine will and human autonomy is called into question. As first noted by the medieval exegete Rashbam (Rabbi Samuel ben Meir, 12th century French scholar and grandson of Rashi), and much later by the 20th century exegete Umberto Cassuto and others, the story of Jacob at Jabok and the story of Moses at the lodging place in Exodus chapter 4 are connected by similar storyline and by idio-syncratic detail. Moses, like Jacob, is confronted by a threatening divine presence on the eve of a great confrontation with former family (Esau and Pharaoh) who have threatened to kill them. In both cases, a dramatic ac-tion, involving the leg of the protagonist, wards off the mysterious threat. The minor injury seems to substitute for the much more serious threat. Even similar language is used in describing this injury:

"**Vayiga** b'caf yereikho" (he touched the hip at the socket). (Gen. 32:26)

"**Vataga** l'raglav" (she caused it to touch his legs). (Exodus 4:25)

The following essay will pursue a close reading of Exodus 4, focusing on the cryptic verses (24–26) that have been described by many scholars as one of the most perplexing and mysterious passages in the Bible.

We join the narrative in chapter two of Exodus, where Moses has already fled Egypt after having killed an Egyptian who was abusing a Hebrew slave. He has settled with Jethro, the Midianite priest, and has married Jethro's daughter Tziporah who has given birth to two sons. In chapter three, God has appeared to Moses at the miraculous burning bush and has charged Moses with the mission of freeing the enslaved nation of Israel from Egyptian bondage. In chapter 4, after repeated protestations on the part of Moses as to his unsuitability for the task, Moses is promised the help of a wondrous staff with which to impress both Pharoah and the Hebrews. He then takes leave of Jethro, receives his blessing, and departs for Egypt with his wife and two sons. The strange interlude at the lodging place is described in the following verses:

> 24) And it came to pass on the way, in the place where they spent the night, that the Lord met him, and sought to kill him.
> 25) Then Tziporah took a sharp stone, and cut off the foreskin of her son, and cast it at his feet, and said: "Surely, a bloody bridegroom art thou to me."
> 26) So He released him: and then she said, "A bloody bridegroom thou art, because of the circumcision." (Ex. 4:24–26)

כד) וַיְהִי בַדֶּרֶךְ בַּמָּלוֹן וַיִּפְגְּשֵׁהוּ יְ-הֹוָה וַיְבַקֵּשׁ הֲמִיתוֹ
כה) וַתִּקַּח צִפֹּרָה צֹר וַתִּכְרֹת אֶת עָרְלַת בְּנָהּ וַתַּגַּע לְרַגְלָיו וַתֹּאמֶר כִּי

148

חֲתַן דָּמִים אַתָּה לִי

כו) וַיִּרֶף מִמֶּנּוּ אָז אָמְרָה חֲתַן דָּמִים לַמּוּלֹת

The biblical story then continues with Moses' return to Egypt as if nothing had interrupted its flow, as the following verse describes Moses' meeting up with his brother Aaron. Aside from the contextual detachment of the episode at the *malon* (lodging place), this compact scene leaves the reader with numerous questions.

Whom does God seek to kill? Is it Moses, Gershom, the oldest, or Eliezer, the younger of the two sons? Why is Tziporah the one to take action? She is, by all accounts, a secondary character in the book of Exodus and is not, as far as we know, invested with prophetic powers. We would have expected Moses the prophet to intuit the danger, to perceive God's threatening hand and for him to take action, or to instruct his wife to do so.

Why is God angry, and in what way does the emergency circumcision assuage the divine wrath? Why is the circumcised son referred to as "her son" and not identified as Gershom or Eliezer, as the older or younger, or for that matter as "his son" or "their son," instead of the partisan בנה. What are the meanings of Tziporah's cryptic pronouncements, both prior to the release of the menacing divine malice (verse 25), and after in the revised pronouncement of verse 26? In the phrase, "she cast it toward [or caused it to touch] his legs," is it the blood, the foreskin, or the makeshift knife that is thrust, and toward whose legs —toward those of the menacing divine presence, of Moses, or of one of the two sons? Ambiguities abound and the cumulative result is a passage as opaque as any in the Hebrew Bible.

Traditional commentaries have focused on the questions of God's motive for the attack, the idea of circumcision as an antidote to God's wrath, and the identity of the circumcised son. In addressing the first question,

Rashi, following the suggestion of the Midrash[1] and the Talmud,[2] suggests that God's wrath was directed toward Moses' failure to circumcise his son. If this were the case, the brith milah (circumcision) would quite naturally be the solution to their sudden distress. The midrash goes so far as to suggest that Moses had concluded a deal with his father-in-law Jethro, a Midianite priest, in which the first born would be raised as a pagan and only subsequent progeny would be dedicated to the God of Israel. Surprisingly, this seemingly preposterous notion does have various textual supports. The Midrash Mekhilta cites the language "ויואל משה לשבת את האיש"—"*Moses undertook* to stay with the man" (Ex. 2:21), as a hint at some sort of oath (אלה) involved in Moses' agreement to dwell with Jethro.[3]

In addition, Rabbi Yitzhak Karo, a sixteenth century Spanish exegete, comments (in his introduction to Exodus 18:3–4) on the absence of God's name in the naming of the first of the two sons. It is the second son, Eliezer, who is named for "the help of the God of my father,"[4] whereas the older son Gershom's naming (Ger = stranger or gentile) is connected to Moses' status as a helpless stranger in an alien land. Additionally, Karo notes the unusual formula used in the verse that introduces Moses' two sons—Gershom and Eliezer—in Exodus chapter 18. Verses three and four speak of "שם האחד... ושם האחד" (the name of the one. . . and the name of the one) in lieu of the more customary "שם האחד... ושם השני" (the name of the first. . . and the name of the second), indicating perhaps that the first-born was indeed under the sole guidance of Jethro and Tziporah whereas the

---

[1] *Mekhilta Yitro, Parasha* 1.

[2] Babylonian Talmud, *Tractate Nedarim* 31a—b.

[3] This finds support as well elsewhere in the Bible as the only other place where this phrase appears in almost identical language, is Judges 17:11: ויואל הלוי לשבת את האיש—"and the Levite undertook to dwell with the man"—this also in the context of the agreement of an idol worshipper to dwell with another. Recall as well that Moses was a Levite. See as well chapter seven, note 11 above, regarding the identification of the Levite as a descendent of Moses.

[4] The Hebrew *Eli* = "my God"; *Ezer* = "help."

second was entrusted to Moses.[5] Hence, each son is *first;* Gershom to the mother—Tziporah, and Eliezer to the father—Moses.[6] We must also note the appearance of an idol-worshipper descending from Moses through his first-born according to the rabbinic understanding of Judges 18:30.[7]

If indeed the uncircumcised son is to be identified as the older Gershom, this Midrash would then offer an opportune connection to the verses preceding the scene at the lodging place: "And you shall say to Pharaoh, 'Thus says the Lord, Yisrael is my son, my first-born.' And I say to you, 'send forth my first born, and you have refused to send him forth —behold I will kill your first born'" (Ex. 4:22–23). In accordance with the Midrash, we should not read this verse as a continuation of an internal quote—i.e., Moses warning Pharaoh about the slaying of the first-born of Egypt. We would rather read it as a direct statement from God to Moses ("and I have said to you"—switching from *God to Pharaoh* to *God to Moses*), admonishing him for his neglect in dedicating his own first-born to God's service, that is, by neglecting to circumcise him. The warning "Behold I will kill your first born son" would then refer to Moses' son and would lead directly to "ויבקש המיתו" ("and He sought to kill him") in the following verse at the lodging place.[8]

In fact, through the ambiguous pronouns and odd syntax used in Exodus 4:22–23, multiple possibilities arise. Consider again the verses quoted above:

Verse 22) "Then you shall say to Pharaoh: "Thus says the Lord: 'My firstborn son is Israel.'

---

[5] See Yitzchak Karo (16th cent.) *Toldot Yitzkhak* (Jerusalem: Makor Press, 1978) on Ex. 18:3–4.

[6] This will be potentially significant in explaining why the circumcised child is referred to as "her son" and why it is that Tziporah must perform the circumcision. Moses either does not possess the necessary parental control over Gershom, or alternatively, needs Tziporah to release him from his "oath."

[7] See Babylonian Talmud, Tractate *Bava Batra* 109b.

[8] See R. Joseph Kimche (13th cent.), *Sefer HaGalui* (Berlin: 1887) 68, s.v. אז.

Verse 23) And I have said to *you,* "send forth my son that he may serve me, and you have refused to send him forth, behold I will kill your firstborn son."

Most plainly, God has described Israel as His first-born in direct analogy to Pharaoh's first-born in order to drive home to Pharaoh the intimacy of the relationship and the affront to God of his crimes against the Israelites. Yet, if the divine threat in verse 24 refers to Moses' first born, the message of verse 23, becomes quite different. You, Moses, have to be sensitized to God's own pain and the urgency of your mission, by learning what it means to have your own first-born in danger. (This level of meaning becomes especially poignant in the context of Moses' repeated reluctance in accepting the mission, as we shall discuss later in the chapter. By bringing his own wife and children, and putting them on the lone donkey while he walks [v. 20], Moses has further delayed the redemption of Israel). Alternatively (and perhaps additionally), according to the Midrash's interpretation (namely, that Moses' first-born is more of a Midianite than a Jew), Moses is being told in verse 23 that he cannot send forth the children of Israel unless he has first tied his own family's destiny to that of the nation. Verse 24 would then put Moses' own first born in a danger more acute than that of Egyptian bondage, the only solution being a bloody and symbolic covenant that ties the son aptly described as בנה—"her son"—to the Israelite nation.

Yet another level offered (if the text were indeed to be read as ambiguous), is the requirement that Moses experience the endangerment of his own son, not only in order to empathize with God, but in order to identify with Pharaoh before confronting him. The hesitant Moses will only fully appreciate his own power when he personally simulates and anticipates the powerlessness of his fearsome adversary in the future slaying of Pharaoh's first-born.

Nevertheless, the explanation of the above midrash leaves several of our questions unanswered and it is to the commentary of the twelfth century exegete Rashbam that we direct our attention. To fully appreciate Rashbam's approach one must examine the end of Exodus Chapter Three and the beginning of Chapter Four. These verses comprise God's instructions to Moses as the liberator of the Israelites from Egypt. In 3:11, Moses' first reaction to God's entrusting him with the mission to save the Israelites is, "Who am I to go before Pharaoh. . . ?"

In chapter 4, verse 1, Moses again questions his own ability to convince the Israelites, let alone Pharaoh, of the authenticity of his mission. God responds with the wonders and signs that He will provide to help Moses make his case. Yet, in verse 10, Moses continues to protest his calling:

בִּי אֲדֹנָי לֹא אִישׁ דְּבָרִים אָנֹכִי גַּם מִתְּמוֹל גַּם מִשִּׁלְשֹׁם גַּם מֵאָז דַּבֶּרְךָ אֶל עַבְדֶּךָ כִּי כְבַד פֶּה וּכְבַד לָשׁוֹן אָנֹכִי

". . . Please my Lord, I am not a man of words, neither yesterday, nor the day before, nor since you spoke to your servant, for heavy of mouth and heavy of tongue am I." (Ex. 4:10)[9]

God's response to Moses' attempt to be absolved of his responsibility carries a distinct tone of building anger:

יא) וַיֹּאמֶר יְ-הֹוָה אֵלָיו מִי שָׂם פֶּה לָאָדָם אוֹ מִי יָשׂוּם אִלֵּם אוֹ חֵרֵשׁ אוֹ פִקֵּחַ אוֹ עִוֵּר הֲלֹא אָנֹכִי יְ-הֹוָה יב) וְעַתָּה לֵךְ וְאָנֹכִי אֶהְיֶה עִם פִּיךָ וְהוֹרֵיתִיךָ אֲשֶׁר תְּדַבֵּר

---

[9] The repetition of the word *"gam"* (*also*, or *neither* or *nor*) in the context of "heavy of mouth and heavy of tongue," may be the source for the Rabbinic, medieval, and modern Hebrew term for stuttering—*"gimgum."* This term is often used as a synonym for uncertainty in speech and in writing. (See Thesaurus Eliezer Ben Yehuda s.v. *gimgum, gamgem*.) In any case, the relationship between lack of self-confidence and reticence to speak on one hand and stammering as a physical manifestation of the psychological state on the other, is clear in the literary description of Moses.

"And God spoke to him: Who has given man a mouth, or who has made him mute or dumb or seeing or blind, am I not God?! And now go, and I will be with your mouth and I will show you what you will say." (Ex. 4:11–12)

Moses is to understand that his physical impediment and its corresponding psychological hesitation are irrelevant in the context of a divine mission. God, who can make the dumb speak or the eloquent speechless, can certainly redeem His people through the agency of one who stutters.

Nonetheless, Moses responds with yet another plea against his appointment as God's messenger, to which God responds with unequivocal anger and a begrudging agreement to appoint Moses' brother Aaron as his mouthpiece:

יג) וַיֹּאמֶר בִּי אֲדֹנָי שְׁלַח נָא בְּיַד תִּשְׁלָח

יד) וַיִּחַר אַף יְ-הֹוָה בְּמֹשֶׁה וַיֹּאמֶר הֲלֹא אַהֲרֹן אָחִיךָ הַלֵּוִי יָדַעְתִּי כִּי דַבֵּר יְדַבֵּר הוּא וְגַם הִנֵּה הוּא יֹצֵא לִקְרָאתֶךָ וְרָאֲךָ וְשָׂמַח בְּלִבּוֹ

טו) וְדִבַּרְתָּ אֵלָיו וְשַׂמְתָּ אֶת הַדְּבָרִים בְּפִיו וְאָנֹכִי אֶהְיֶה עִם פִּיךָ וְעִם פִּיהוּ וְהוֹרֵיתִי אֶתְכֶם אֵת אֲשֶׁר תַּעֲשׂוּן

טז) וְדִבֶּר הוּא לְךָ אֶל הָעָם וְהָיָה הוּא יִהְיֶה לְּךָ לְפֶה וְאַתָּה תִּהְיֶה לּוֹ לֵאלֹהִים

יז) וְאֶת הַמַּטֶּה הַזֶּה תִּקַּח בְּיָדֶךָ אֲשֶׁר תַּעֲשֶׂה בּוֹ אֶת הָאֹתֹת

"But he said, 'please Lord, pray send someone else as your messenger.'

And the Lord became angry with Moses and He said, 'Is it not Aaron your brother the Levite whom I know will readily speak and even now he is going out towards you, and he will see you and will be glad in his heart.

You shall speak to him and shall put the words in his mouth and

I will be with your mouth and with his mouth and I will instruct
you as to what you will do.
And he shall speak for you to the people and it shall be that he will
be for you a mouthpiece and you will be for him as a lord.
And this staff take in your hand that you might perform with it
the signs.'"
(Ex. 4:13–17)

Henceforth, Moses is to lead the people while supported by two crutch-
es, Aaron's oratory at one side and the wondrous staff at the other.

Rashi and Rashbam are both concerned with the anomalous appearance
of God's wrath ("ויחר אף"), in verse 14, without an accompanying consequence. Elsewhere in the Bible, divine wrath is always followed by practical result, be it epidemic, failure in battle or other forms of punishment.
Without a tangible consequence, God's anger remains an unacceptable
anthropomorphism as well as a literary anomaly in biblical style for the
medieval exegetes. (For these exegetes, the reason that divine anger will
always have a practical result is that the "anger" only has meaning as understood from the human experience of punishment—God himself being
above the mundane, mortal, constrictions of emotions such as anger.)

Rashi solves this anomaly by suggesting that the resulting punishment of
Moses was that mentioned in the very same verse (4:14), namely that Aaron
would share the leadership. Yet, it is difficult to view this as a punishment
as Moses is clearly asking God to divest him of responsibility. Removal
from the limelight is more of a reward for Moses than a punishment.

Perhaps because of the above difficulty, Rashbam takes issue with his
grandfather Rashi and offers a novel solution. He suggests that the punishment ensuing from the unspecified wrath ("חרון אף") in verse 14 is
none other than the attack on Moses in verse 24.[10] The initial impetus for

---

[10] Support for identifying the ambiguous pronoun in the phrase "ויבקש המיתו—He
[God] **sought to kill** *him*" (Ex. 4:24) as Moses, may be found by comparing this

Rashbam's proposal must have been the coincidence and close proximity of a crime in search of a punishment in one verse, and a mysterious punishment in search of a crime in the other.

It would indeed provide a tidy solution to a double problem if the attack on Moses at the night's lodging was a response to his inappropriate humility in refusing God's mission. But Rashbam leaves no indication as to the intrinsic connection between circumcision and Moses' misguided concern about being *heavy of tongue*. If, as Rashbam suggests, the threat at the *malon* was a consequence of Moses' inappropriate reluctance to speak, in what way was circumcision the response that succeeded in defusing the divine anger?

On a conceptual plane, one might suggest that circumcision symbolizes the idea that an apparent detraction from the perfection of nature, when ordained by God, can actually be positive or advantageous. In a play on the commercial wisdom that "less is more," particularly when "less" represents God's will, the surgical procedure may be seen as a detraction from the body, but at the same time, a sign of being chosen, and a dedication of spiritual significance. The circumcision, then, was to teach Moses that his apparent disability or imperfection as a stammerer not only did not disqualify him as a spokesman, but may have been one of the reasons that God had chosen him.

Both Ibn Ezra[11] and Malbim[12] in their comments on Exodus 4:14, suggest in different ways that God had a distinct reason for wanting his message to be presented by a stutterer. According to Malbim, the peoples of Israel and Egypt were to attribute the Exodus exclusively to God, and not to a charismatic leader. The subsequent delegation of public speaking to Aaron was therefore an undesirable concession to Moses, detracting

---

verse with Ex. 4:19 "כי מתו כל האנשים המבקשים את נפשך"—where it is Moses who is told in similar words "the *people* who **sought to kill** you are dead."

[11] A 12th century Spanish exegete—Abraham Ibn Ezra.

[12] A 19th century exegete—Rabbi Meir ben Leibush (Ukraine, Poland, Rumania).

from God's original intention. One might bring support for this understanding—of God's wrath at a Moses who detracts from the sanctification of God's name—from a parallel passage in Numbers 20:7–13:

> "And God spoke to Moses saying, 'Take the **staff** and gather together the community, you and **Aaron** your brother and **speak to the rock** before their eyes and it will give forth its waters'. . . And Moses raised his hand and **struck the rock** twice with his staff and much water came forth and the community and their animals drank. And God said to Moses and to Aaron, 'Because you have not trusted me to sanctify me before the eyes of the children of Israel, therefore you will not bring this congregation to the land that I have given them.' "

In both passages, God becomes angry with Moses for failing to speak—instead relying on the staff in the latter instance and on the oratory of Aaron in the former. In the latter case, the text makes explicit the reason for anger—the failure to maximize the sanctification of God in the eyes of the people. So too, for Malbim and Ibn Ezra, by insisting on his own inadequacy and prying the concession of Aaron as spokesman, Moses has diminished the potential for sanctifying God.

Though Rashbam fails to note it, textual proof for his explanation and for our suggested conceptual link between circumcision and Moses' speech impediment, is the startling synonym for "heavy of tongue" used later in Exodus 6:12 and Ex. 6:30:

וַיֹּאמֶר מֹשֶׁה לִפְנֵי יְ-הֹוָה הֵן אֲנִי עֲרַל שְׂפָתַיִם וְאֵיךְ יִשְׁמַע אֵלַי פַּרְעֹה

> "And Moses said before the Lord, Behold I am **uncircumcised of lips** and how shall Pharaoh hear me?"

157

Considering the use of "ערל שפתיים—*uncircumcised of lips*"—as a synonym for stuttering, it is not far-fetched to conclude that the circumcision at the *malon* is to be understood as an attempt to simultaneously and symbolically remove "ערלת השפתיים" (the foreskin of the lips) from the hesitant Moses who has incurred God's wrath by his obstinate reluctance to speak. Rashbam's clever pairing of 4:14 (God's anger at Moses' inability to transcend his sense of heavy mouth and tongue), and 4:24–26 (the divine attack at the *malon* and the antidote of circumcision), has thus received persuasive literary support from the idiosyncratic paraphrase of *heavy tongue* in the term—*uncircumcised of lips.*

Further textual indication of the connection between 4:14 and 4:24–26 is the undeniable parallel between the words that immediately follow each of these verses. In verse 4:14, God's anger is followed by the words, "behold **Aaron** your brother the Levite, I have known that he will surely speak and here he comes **out toward you**. . ." Immediately following the episode at the *malon*, the very next words are, "And God said to **Aaron**: 'go **out toward** Moses. . .'"(4:27).

Moreover, the connection between the two passages and the underscoring of Moses' inappropriate reluctance to carry out God's mission is conveyed not only by the epilogue to the *malon* story, but by its prologue as well. In verses 4:18-21 we read:

> 18) And Moses **went** and **returned** to Jethro his father-in-law and said to him, "pray thee I will **go** and **return** to my brothers who are in Egypt and I will see if they are still alive"—and Jethro said, "go in peace."
>
> 19) And the Lord said to Moses in Midian, "**Go, return** to Egypt for all the people who seek your life have died."
>
> 20) And Moses took his wife and his sons and he placed them up upon the donkey and he **returned** to the land of Egypt, and Moses took the staff of God with him.

21) And the Lord said to Moses, "as you **go** to **return** to Egypt, regard these wonders that I have placed in your hands and you shall perform them before Pharaoh and I will strengthen his heart and he will not send forth the nation."

יח) וַיֵּלֶךְ מֹשֶׁה וַיָּשָׁב אֶל יֶתֶר חֹתְנוֹ וַיֹּאמֶר לוֹ אֵלְכָה נָּא וְאָשׁוּבָה אֶל אַחַי אֲשֶׁר בְּמִצְרַיִם וְאֶרְאֶה הַעוֹדָם חַיִּים וַיֹּאמֶר יִתְרוֹ לְמֹשֶׁה לֵךְ לְשָׁלוֹם

יט) וַיֹּאמֶר יְ-הֹוָה אֶל מֹשֶׁה בְּמִדְיָן לֵךְ שֻׁב מִצְרָיִם כִּי מֵתוּ כָּל הָאֲנָשִׁים הַמְבַקְשִׁים אֶת נַפְשֶׁךָ

כ) וַיִּקַּח מֹשֶׁה אֶת אִשְׁתּוֹ וְאֶת בָּנָיו וַיַּרְכִּבֵם עַל הַחֲמֹר וַיָּשָׁב אַרְצָה מִצְרָיִם וַיִּקַּח מֹשֶׁה אֶת מַטֵּה הָאֱ-לֹהִים בְּיָדוֹ

כא) וַיֹּאמֶר יְ-הֹוָה אֶל מֹשֶׁה בְּלֶכְתְּךָ לָשׁוּב מִצְרַיְמָה רְאֵה כָּל הַמֹּפְתִים אֲשֶׁר שַׂמְתִּי בְיָדֶךָ וַעֲשִׂיתָם לִפְנֵי פַרְעֹה וַאֲנִי אֲחַזֵּק אֶת לִבּוֹ וְלֹא יְשַׁלַּח אֶת הָעָם

Prior to these verses, in chapter three, God had already commanded Moses to go (*lekh, lekha*) to Egypt.[13] Now Moses comes to Jethro and seeks his permission or blessing to "**go** and to **return**." Yet after receiving Jethro's "**go** in peace," the next verse does not proceed with the expected "and Moses went." Instead, God commands Moses yet again to "**go** and **return**" (*lekh, shuv*).[14]

In verse 20, Moses **returns** (*vayashov*) to Egypt; however, both the syntax and language of the verse indicate a return that is ambivalent and

---

[13] See Ex. 3:10, 17.

[14] I am reminded of a cartoon I saw many years ago in which a suburban couple stand at the door of their home waving goodbye to another couple about to enter their car. The wife turns to the husband and says, "They must not have had a very good time. They left right after they said goodbye." Notwithstanding the phenomenon of prolonged goodbyes, and particularly in the economic language of biblical narrative, after Moses takes his leave and Jethro says, "Go in peace," we fully expect Moses to go. We therefore discern a purposeful literary ploy when, instead, God must yet again tell Moses to go.

halting. The structure of the verse is odd in that first we are told of the preparations for the journey—specifically the "taking" (*vayikach*) of his wife and sons. The middle of the verse states "and he returned." The end of the verse reverts to the preparations for the journey—specifically the "taking" *(vayikach)* of the staff of God. In addition, this verse contains a break with the pattern of language used to describe Moses' movements. Four times in these four verses Moses or God or the narrative voice describe Moses as both **returning** and **going**. However, in verse 20, Moses is described as "returning" (*vayashov*) without "going" (*vayelekh*).

The text has underscored the paradox of a return without locomotion, both by creating an expectation of double verbiage and then departing from the pattern and by structuring the verse as a dance in which there are two steps forward and one back. Clearly, form has reflected substance in this regard as the verse informs us that Moses has chosen to bring his wife and two young sons with him to Egypt, a questionable decision that will hinder the speed of his return.[15] In addition, we are informed that there is only one donkey and that Moses has placed the wife and sons on the donkey while he proceeds on foot alongside them. Just as there is coffee without caffeine, so too there can be a journey without locomotion, *returning* without *going*.

Moreover, this halting progress, this syntactical forward motion that takes an occasional detour or "about face," continues in the next verse. Though all the preparations and instructions for the journey have *prima facie* been given, and the past tense has already been used to say, "and Moses returned," verse 21 takes us back to the starting point as God tells Moses what it is that he should be considering as he goes and returns to Egypt (*"b'lekhtekha lashuv"* as if the text has not already stated *"vayashav"*).

---

[15] That the escort of his family was a mistaken decision rectified at the *malon*, is implied both by the absence of Tzipora and sons after the episode at the *malon* in the story of the Exodus, and by Ex. 18:2—in which we are told that Jethro hears of the Exodus after the fact and comes out to meet Moses with Tzipora and the two boys "after her being sent away" (*achar shilucheha*).

The reticence indicated in these verses that lead up to the scene at the *malon*, is significant not only as it affects a time delay in carrying out God's plan, but primarily in the way it threatens to affect the manner in which the mission will be undertaken. An urgent and dramatic act of deliverance cannot be performed without a sense of urgency and drama. The cumulative effect of this ambivalent dance of forward backward progress is the further literary confirmation of Rashbam's contention. Proceeding from Rashbam's observation, the episode at the *malon* may be seen as the pivotal moment of transition in an internal struggle that involves Moses' insecurities and his reluctance to accept the divine mission.

Yet perhaps most intriguing in Rashbam's approach is his comment elsewhere in his Torah commentary (Gen. 32:29), concerning Jacob's wrestling with the man/angel on the eve of his confrontation with Esau:

> "...And with regard to Jacob's wound and subsequent limp, it is because God had assured him, yet he was fleeing. And so we find with all those who walk their path against the will of God, or refuse to walk, that they are punished. With regard to Moses it is written 'Send whomever you send [just not me], and God waxed angry with Moses' (Ex. 4:24). And according to the plain meaning (even though the Sages stated that in every instance divine anger must provide consequence and the consequence here is that Aaron your brother was destined to be the Levite and you the priest but now he will be the priest and you the Levite), the plain meaning is that he was reluctant to go and on the way to the lodging place, He met him and sought to kill him. So it was with Jonah swallowed into the belly of the fish (Jonah 2:1). And thus with Baalam: 'and the Lord waxed angry that he went' (Num. 22:22) and he became lame as it is written 'and Baalam's leg was pressed [against the wall]' (Num. 22:25), 'and he walked lamely' (Num. 23:3)."[16]

---

[16] *Peirush Hatorah Rashbam* (ed. David Rosin) (Breslau: Stadtlander Press, 1882)

Even at first glance, the comparison between the Jacob, Moses, and Baalam stories is striking. In each story a divine presence attacks the hero on the eve of a great confrontation. Jacob walks away limping, Baalam's leg is pressed to the wall and he walks away lame, and Moses is released only after his son's foreskin is cast toward his leg.[17] In both the Moses and the Jacob stories, the verb used to describe the action performed upon the leg is the verb **נגע** ("**ויגע בגף ירכו**"in Gen. 32:26 and "**ותגע לרגליו**" in Exodus 4:25).

Yet upon further examination, it is the comparison between the Baalam story and that of Moses on the way to Egypt that will be particularly apt and astonishingly fruitful. Notwithstanding Ibn Ezra's objection (Ex. 4:14, s.v. ויחר אף) to Rashbam's comparison between Moses and Baalam as misguided—as Moses went at God's bidding and Baalam did not—the literary parallel between the two stories is extensive, as we shall demonstrate. Moreover, given God's eventual permission to Baalam to accompany Balak's ministers (in Numbers 22:20), it is much more accurate to state that Baalam provoked God's anger not by his going, but in his inappropriate eagerness to go. Much in the same way, Moses provokes God not by ultimately refusing to go, but in his inappropriate reluctance to go.[18]

On the surface, Ibn Ezra is quite correct in rejecting a simplistic equation of Baalam and Moses. However, I believe Rashbam's comments point

---

Gen. 32:29, s.v. *ki sarita*. (The translation is my own—S.K.)

[17] According to an entirely feasible interpretation of Ex. 4:25 in *Talmud Yerushalmi* (*Nedarim* Ch. 3 Halakha 9) as understood by the Talmudic commentary *Korban Ha'edah*, Tziporah did not "cast the foreskin at his feet" but rather "ותגע לרגליו" is to be translated—"and she nicked his legs"—accidentally wounding him with her knife, due to the speed and panic surrounding the surgery. This explanation accounts for the revised pronouncement of verses 25 and 26 (first, "חתן דמים אתה לי" and then "חתן דמים למולות") as well as providing a sharper parallel to the Baalam and Jacob incidents where the leg is actually wounded to indicate a failing in the manner ("דרך") in which they are about to walk.

[18] This has also been noted by Joshua Blau in his article, "*Chatan Damim*"in *Tarbiz*, Tishrei 5617 (Jerusalem: Magnes Press, 1957) 1–3.

to the possibility of a more complex parallel than the one that either
Rashbam himself or Ibn Ezra had in mind. This comparison will portray
an inverse or *mirror* parallel of men with contrasting dispositions that
require opposite remedies. Before demonstrating the inverse nature of
the parallel, we will list the numerous literary similarities that lead one
to the inescapable conclusion that we are dealing with twin stories—with
Scripture fully explicating the cryptic episode at the night's lodging (Ex. 4)
by means of its intertextual relation to the Baalam story (Num. 22)[19].

In Numbers 22:16–35, after Baalam's initial refusal of the request of
Balak that he accompany him and curse the Israelite nation, we read:

(טז) וַיָּבֹאוּ אֶל בִּלְעָם וַיֹּאמְרוּ לוֹ כֹּה אָמַר בָּלָק **בֶּן צִפּוֹר** אַל נָא תִמָּנַע
מֵהֲלֹךְ אֵלָי:

(יז) כִּי **כַבֵּד אֲכַבֶּדְךָ** מְאֹד וְכֹל אֲשֶׁר תֹּאמַר אֵלַי אֶעֱשֶׂה וּלְכָה נָּא קָבָה
לִּי אֵת הָעָם הַזֶּה:

(יח) וַיַּעַן בִּלְעָם וַיֹּאמֶר אֶל עַבְדֵי בָלָק אִם יִתֶּן לִי בָלָק מְלֹא בֵיתוֹ
כֶּסֶף וְזָהָב לֹא אוּכַל לַעֲבֹר אֶת פִּי יְ־הֹוָה אֱלֹהָי לַעֲשׂוֹת קְטַנָּה אוֹ
גְדוֹלָה:

(יט) וְעַתָּה שְׁבוּ נָא בָזֶה גַּם אַתֶּם הַלָּיְלָה וְאֵדְעָה מַה יֹּסֵף יְ־הֹוָה דַּבֵּר
עִמִּי:

(כ) וַיָּבֹא אֱ־לֹהִים אֶל בִּלְעָם לַיְלָה וַיֹּאמֶר לוֹ אִם לִקְרֹא לְךָ בָּאוּ
הָאֲנָשִׁים קוּם לֵךְ אִתָּם וְאַךְ אֶת הַדָּבָר אֲשֶׁר אֲדַבֵּר אֵלֶיךָ אֹתוֹ
תַעֲשֶׂה:

(כא) וַיָּקָם בִּלְעָם בַּבֹּקֶר וַיַּחֲבֹשׁ אֶת **אֲתֹנוֹ** וַיֵּלֶךְ עִם שָׂרֵי מוֹאָב:

(כב) **וַיִּחַר אַף אֱ־לֹהִים** כִּי הוֹלֵךְ הוּא וַיִּתְיַצֵּב מַלְאַךְ יְ־הֹוָה **בַּדֶּרֶךְ**
לְשָׂטָן לוֹ וְהוּא רֹכֵב עַל אֲתֹנוֹ **וּשְׁנֵי נְעָרָיו** עִמּוֹ:

(כג) וַתֵּרֶא הָאָתוֹן אֶת מַלְאַךְ יְ־הֹוָה נִצָּב **בַּדֶּרֶךְ** וְחַרְבּוֹ שְׁלוּפָה בְּיָדוֹ
וַתֵּט הָאָתוֹן מִן **הַדֶּרֶךְ** וַתֵּלֶךְ בַּשָּׂדֶה וַיַּךְ בִּלְעָם אֶת הָאָתוֹן לְהַטֹּתָהּ

---

[19] See the comment of the Palestinian Talmud (Tractate Rosh Hashana 3:5)
concerning Proverbs 31:14: 'The words of Torah are poor in their own location
and rich elsewhere.'

הַדָּרֶךְ:

(כד) וַיַּעֲמֹד מַלְאַךְ יְ-הֹוָה בְּמִשְׁעוֹל הַכְּרָמִים גָּדֵר מִזֶּה וְגָדֵר מִזֶּה:

(כה) וַתֵּרֶא הָאָתוֹן אֶת מַלְאַךְ יְ-הֹוָה וַתִּלָּחֵץ אֶל הַקִּיר **וַתִּלְחַץ אֶת רֶגֶל בִּלְעָם** אֶל הַקִּיר וַיֹּסֶף לְהַכֹּתָהּ:

(כו) וַיּוֹסֶף מַלְאַךְ יְ-הֹוָה עֲבוֹר וַיַּעֲמֹד בְּמָקוֹם **צָר** אֲשֶׁר אֵין **דֶּרֶךְ** לִנְטוֹת יָמִין וּשְׂמֹאול:

(כז) וַתֵּרֶא הָאָתוֹן אֶת מַלְאַךְ יְ-הֹוָה וַתִּרְבַּץ תַּחַת בִּלְעָם וַיִּחַר אַף בִּלְעָם וַיַּךְ אֶת הָאָתוֹן בַּמַּקֵּל:

(כח) **וַיִּפְתַּח יְ-הֹוָה אֶת פִּי הָאָתוֹן** וַתֹּאמֶר לְבִלְעָם מֶה עָשִׂיתִי לְךָ כִּי הִכִּיתַנִי זֶה שָׁלֹשׁ רְגָלִים:

(כט) וַיֹּאמֶר בִּלְעָם לָאָתוֹן כִּי הִתְעַלַּלְתְּ בִּי לוּ יֶשׁ חֶרֶב בְּיָדִי כִּי עַתָּה הֲרַגְתִּיךְ:

(ל) וַתֹּאמֶר הָאָתוֹן אֶל בִּלְעָם הֲלוֹא אָנֹכִי אֲתֹנְךָ אֲשֶׁר רָכַבְתָּ עָלַי מֵעוֹדְךָ עַד הַיּוֹם הַזֶּה הַהַסְכֵּן הִסְכַּנְתִּי לַעֲשׂוֹת לְךָ כֹּה וַיֹּאמֶר לֹא:

(לא) וַיְגַל יְ-הֹוָה אֶת עֵינֵי בִלְעָם וַיַּרְא אֶת מַלְאַךְ יְ-הֹוָה נִצָּב בַּדֶּרֶךְ וְחַרְבּוֹ שְׁלֻפָה בְּיָדוֹ וַיִּקֹּד וַיִּשְׁתַּחוּ לְאַפָּיו:

(לב) וַיֹּאמֶר אֵלָיו מַלְאַךְ יְ-הֹוָה עַל מָה הִכִּיתָ אֶת אֲתֹנְךָ זֶה שָׁלוֹשׁ רְגָלִים הִנֵּה אָנֹכִי יָצָאתִי לְשָׂטָן כִּי יָרַט הַדֶּרֶךְ לְנֶגְדִּי:

(לג) וַתִּרְאַנִי הָאָתוֹן וַתֵּט לְפָנַי זֶה שָׁלֹשׁ רְגָלִים אוּלַי נָטְתָה מִפָּנַי כִּי עַתָּה גַּם **אֹתְכָה הָרַגְתִּי** וְאוֹתָהּ הֶחֱיֵיתִי:

(לד) וַיֹּאמֶר בִּלְעָם אֶל מַלְאַךְ יְ-הֹוָה חָטָאתִי כִּי לֹא יָדַעְתִּי כִּי אַתָּה נִצָּב לִקְרָאתִי בַּדָּרֶךְ וְעַתָּה אִם רַע בְּעֵינֶיךָ אָשׁוּבָה לִּי:

(לה) וַיֹּאמֶר מַלְאַךְ יְ-הֹוָה אֶל בִּלְעָם לֵךְ עִם הָאֲנָשִׁים וְאֶפֶס אֶת הַדָּבָר אֲשֶׁר אֲדַבֵּר אֵלֶיךָ אֹתוֹ תְדַבֵּר וַיֵּלֶךְ בִּלְעָם עִם שָׂרֵי בָלָק:

16) They came to Baalam and said to him, "Thus says Balak son of Tzipor: Please do not refuse to come to me.

17) I will heavily reward you a great deal,[20] and will do anything

---

[20] I have preferred to translate this phrase in a more awkward literal fashion than the idiomatic JPS translation—"I will reward you richly" (and yet less literally than Fox's translation "I will honor, yes, honor") in order to preserve and underscore the

you request of me; but please come and curse this people for me."

18) But Baalam answered and said to the servants of Balak: "Even if Balak were to give me his house full of silver and gold, I am not able to transgress the word of the Lord my God in small or great matters.

19) And now please also stay here tonight and I will know what the Lord will say to me."

20) And God came to Baalam at night and said to him: "If the men have come to call for you, rise and go with them, but only that which I will say to you will you do."

21) And Baalam rose in the morning and saddled his *aton* (she-ass) and went with the officers of Balak.

22) And God waxed angry that he went and an angel of God took up position on the way as an adversary. And he was riding on his *aton* and his two lads were with him.

23) And the *aton* saw the angel of the Lord positioned on the path, his sword drawn in his hand, and the *aton* swerved from the way and went into the field, and Baalam smote the *aton* to turn it back to the way.

24) And the angel of the Lord stood in the lane among the vineyards, a fence on either side.

25) And the *aton* saw the angel of the Lord and she pressed up against the wall and Baalam's leg pressed against the wall and he continued to beat her.

26) And the angel of the Lord continued to pass and took up position in a narrow space where there was no room to move right or left.

---

relationship between כבד as reward or honor and כבד as heavy. This will, in turn, underscore the literary parallel to the use of כבד פה, כבד לשון (heavy of mouth and tongue) in Exodus 4.

27) And the *aton* saw the angel of the Lord and she collapsed beneath Baalam and Baalam waxed angry and beat the *aton* with the rod.

28) And the Lord opened the mouth of the *aton* and she said to Baalam: "What have I done to you that you have beaten me these three times?"

29) And Baalam said to the *aton*: "For you have mocked me; if I had a sword in my hand I would have already killed you!"

30) And the *aton* said to Baalam: "Am I not your *aton* upon which you have been riding from whenever until this very day? Have I ever endangered you to do something as this?" And he said: "No."

31) And the Lord uncovered Baalam's eyes and he saw the angel of the Lord positioned on the path and his sword drawn in his hand whereupon he bent over and bowed to the ground.

32–33) And the angel of the Lord said to Baalam, "Why have you smitten your *aton*? . . . I was about to kill you and let her live!"

34) And Baalam said to the angel of the Lord: "I have sinned. . . and now if it is evil in your eyes [for me to continue] I will turn back."

35) And the angel of the Lord said to Baalam: "Go with the men, but nothing but that which I will say to you will you speak." And Baalam went with the officers of Balak.

The peculiar instance in the Baalam story of God opening the mouth of the **aton** (she-ass)—female counterpart of the male **hamor** (donkey) in the *malon* story in Exodus—is clearly intended to convey to Baalam the message that prophetic oratory is a divine gift. Baalam had displayed arrogance in presuming prophetic powers of speech that were independent of God's will. In effect, God has said to Baalam, you are nothing but my chosen mouthpiece among the mortals, and if I choose to, I can grant the power of speech and the ability to perceive the metaphysical to a she-ass. Thus, "And God opened the mouth of the *aton*" (Num. 22:28) is a paraphrase of God's admonishing Moses (Ex. 4:12) "who gives mouth to men or who strikes him mute!"

Moses' return to Egypt begins with the verse:

"And Moses took his wife and his sons and placed them upon the *hamor* (donkey) and he returned to the land of Mitzraim. And Moses took the staff of the Lord in his hand." (Ex. 4:20)

כ) וַיִּקַּח מֹשֶׁה אֶת אִשְׁתּוֹ וְאֶת בָּנָיו וַיַּרְכִּבֵם עַל הַחֲמֹר וַיָּשָׁב אַרְצָה מִצְרָיִם וַיִּקַּח מֹשֶׁה אֶת מַטֵּה הָאֱ-לֹהִים בְּיָדוֹ

The authors of the midrash (and Rashi in their footsteps) have pondered the use of the definite article with regard to Moses' donkey. Because of the appearance of "*ha'hamor*" (**the** donkey), which Rabbinic exegetical methodology expected to be "*hamor*" (a donkey) or "*hamoro*" (his donkey), they inferred symbolic significance to the donkey or at the very least, specificity, beyond its functional role as a means of transportation. Various homiletic commentaries have suggested "*hamor*" as a symbol of "*homer*"—material or "*homriut*"—materiality. I shall try to support this view in a moment, though in biblical Hebrew, the word *h-m-r* (חמר) is used to mean clay or dirt, rather than "material," with the possible exception of the word's appearance in Job 13:12.

In any case, there would seem to be an additional parallel here between a particular donkey "ha'hamor" and Baalam's particular she-ass —"ha-aton" (Num. 22:23). Note as well, that Moses proceeds with two sons, as does Baalam with his two lads (Num. 22:22). Scripture makes a point of Moses taking the staff of the Lord "מטה," just as the rod "מקל" (Num. 22:27) plays a role in Baalam's farce with the *aton*. In both stories, people come from Midian with wonders or magic "in their hands" (compare

Ex.4:21 to Numbers 22:7).

In Ex. 4:24, the fact that the divine threat takes place in transit is emphasized by the introductory phrase "ויהי בדרך," "and it happened on the way." In the passage in Numbers 22, the term "בדרך" (on the way), is used twice in verses 22 and 23 and the word "דרך" (way or path) appears five more times in the following verses.

As mentioned above, both stories take place on the eve of a great confrontation and both (according to Rashbam) revolve around the powers of speech of a prophet, in one case an inappropriately humble underestimation and in the other an arrogant overestimation of those powers. Both stories reach their climax with a symbolic act upon the leg of the protagonist, "ותגע לרגליו"—"she cast it towards [or *nicked]* his legs" (Ex. 4:25) and "ותלחץ את רגל בלעם"—"Baalam's leg was pressed [against the wall]" (Num. 22:25).

In both cases, the prophet evokes God's ire: "**ויחר אף ה' במשה**" (Ex. 4:14) and "**ויחר אף א-לוהים**" (Num. 22:22). And in both stories a divine presence threatens to kill the prophet on his way, "מלאך ה' נצב בדרך וחרבו שלופה" (Ex. 4:24) and "ויפגשהו ה' ויבקש המיתו בידו" (Num. 22:23).

The verb **מאן**—*to refuse* or *decline*, is used twice in the Baalam story in describing God's declining to allow Baalam to accompany Balak's emissaries. Similarly, it appears in the verse describing either Moses or Pharaoh's declining to send forth God's first-born in Exodus 4:23, the verse immediately preceding the incident at the *malon*.[21] In the *malon* story, the verb **מאן** is used to denote the human refusal of a divine mandate; in the Baalam story the same word denotes the divine refusal of a human request.

In Rashbam's understanding of the flow of chapter four of Exodus, it is Moses' sense of himself as *"heavy of mouth and heavy of tongue"* "**כבד**

---

[21] The verb **מאן** is not a particularly common word in the Hebrew Bible; in these two parallel stories we find three of the thirteen appearances of this verb in the Pentateuch.

"פה וכבד לשון" that deflates Moses' self-confidence and leads him to his inappropriate reluctance to accept God's mission. Conversely, it is the promise by Balak of material reward and great honor—כבד אכבדך, "*I will heavily honor you*"—that inflates Baalam's ego and leads him to his inappropriate exuberance in accepting a mission contrary to God's will. Underscoring the intertextual reference is the doubling in each verse of the word כבד.[22]

Moreover, the climax of both the scene of the talking *aton* and that of the *malon* share the critical element encapsulated by the word *tz-r*—"צר." In the *malon* scene, Tziporah takes a צר—(*tzor*) a sharp stone with which to circumcise her son in response to the divine threat.[23] In Numbers 22, Baalam and the *aton* are threatened by a divine presence that is perceived only by the *aton*. They literally and literarily reach an impasse when the lane becomes narrow (*tz-r*, צר). It is only at this point that God opens the mouth of the she-ass.

Yet the most peculiar common feature of the two episodes is the following: Baalam exhibits obstinate myopia with regard to the divine threat, while an unexpected secondary character, namely the *aton*, not only perceives the threat but knows how to react. In similar fashion, Moses displays total passivity, perhaps paralysis in the face of the divine threat, while again an unexpected secondary character, namely Tzipora, not only perceives the danger, but intuits the proper response.

The parallels between the two stories (particularly when taking into

---

[22] The same root, כבד, in Hebrew, means *heavy* and *honor*. The relationship between the initial concrete meaning and its presumably later abstract meaning is intuitively evident.

[23] The symbolism of the word *tz-r* may be tied to the general foreshadowing of the exodus from *Mitzraim (same root—tz-r)* in the *malon* scene. This foreshadowing includes casting blood upon the doorposts (similar to this scene's casting of blood at the feet), the requirement of circumcision before eating of the paschal lamb, and, of course, the slaying (or near slaying) of the first-born. Again, historically the two words *tz-r* here may stem from two distinct roots but historical etymology becomes almost irrelevant in a suggestion of syllepsis or wordplay.

account Rashbam's correlation of the lodging incident with Moses' earlier reticence to speak) are too numerous and idiosyncratic to ignore:

MOSES (Exodus 4)	BALAAM (Numbers 22)
בדרך (On the way) (4:24)	בדרך (On the way)—7 times
בלכתך [ממדין] ...ראה כל המפתים אשר שמתי בידך—upon your **journey** [from Midian] consider the **wonders** I have put into your hands (4:21)[24]	**וילכו**—And ...וזקני **מדין וקסמים בידם** the elders of **Midian journeyed** with **magic in their hands** (22:7)
Eve of a great confrontation	Eve of a great confrontation
ויחר אף ה' (And God waxed angry)	ויחר אף א-לוהים (And the Lord waxed angry)
ויפגשהו ה' ויבקש המיתו divine threat to kill (4:24)	מלאך ה' נצב בדרך וחרבו שלופה בידו גם אתכה הרגתי divine threat to kill (22:31, 33)
ותמאן לשלחו And you have **refused** to send him forth (4:23) (human refuses divine mission)	**מאן** י-הוה לתתי להלך עמכם The Lord has **refused** to let me go with you (22:13) (God refuses human mission)
כי **כבד** פה **וכבד** לשון אנכי For I am **heavy** of mouth and **heavy** of tongue (4:10) (therefore I cannot serve as your agent)	**כבד אכבדך** [Do not refuse to come to me for] I will **heavily** (richly) reward you (22:17) (therefore serve as my agent)
מי שם פה לאדם ומי ישום אלם (God) Who gives speech to man or sets one mute (4:11)	ויפתח ה' את פי האתון God opened the mouth of the she-ass (22:28)
החמור the ass (4:20)	**האתון** the she-ass (22:23)
Moses' reticence to perform a mission considered urgent by God (4:10–14)	Balaam's eagerness to perform a mission undesired by God (22:17–20)
prophet underestimates his powers of speech	prophet overestimates his powers of speech
secondary character discerns the divine threat and responds; the protagonist remains passive	secondary character discerns the divine threat and responds; the protagonist remains unaware
ותקח צפרה **צר** And Tzipora took a **tzor** (a sharp stone) (4:25)	ויעמד במקום **צר** And he stood still at a **narrow (tzar)** place (22:26)
ותגע לרגליו "and she nicked his legs" (4:25)	ותלחץ את רגל בלעם אל הקיר and she pressed Balaam's leg against the wall (22:25)
"and Moses took his. . .[two] boys" (4:20)	"and his two lads with him" (22:22)
המטה Moses' staff	המקל Balaam's rod
(בנה) בן **צפורה** ben Tzipora	**בלק בן צפור** Balak (**ben Tzipor**)

170

Once an intended literary parallel is perceived, one may proceed to an understanding of the inverse relationship between the two passages: Baalam's weakness is hubris. He believes he can transcend his role as God's messenger, and can supersede God's will by using his power of speech to curse a blessed people. He is brought down to his true stature by a female donkey—an *aton*, who shows greater prophetic power than Baalam in discerning the angel and delivers God's message faithfully through her miraculous power of speech.[25]

Conversely, Moses' weakness is his humility.[26] He believes that his physical/psychological impediments will prevent him from carrying out God's mission, that his heavy mouth and heavy tongue (Ex. 4:10) should rightfully disqualify him from serving as God's agent. He fears that he will be unable to transcend this heaviness, and will thereby fail to rise to the challenge of redeeming his brothers from bondage. Moses is taught by Tziporah, through the symbolism of *brith milah* (circumcision) that "less is sometimes more," and that God's appointment or command may actually transform a limitation or liability into an advantage.

---

[24] In both verses we find the only appearances in the Bible of "wonders" or "magic" *in the hand*.

[25] The didactic farce is played out even in its details as Baalam who "rough rides" his she-ass, beating her **three times** (Num. 2:28), is ridden, as it were, by Balak, who echoes the exasperation of Baalam with his *aton* when he berates Baalam for the **three times** that God frustrates their efforts to curse the Israelites (Num. 23:10). In the parallel verses, just as Baalam is frustrated because the *aton* does not "provide service," Balak sees the haughty prophet Baalam as a mere provider of services who has failed to supply the goods. The irony of Baalam played by the she-ass thus extends beyond the primary way in which prophetic vision and powers of speech are taken from Baalam and given to his animal.

[26] When the Torah describes Moses as:

"והאיש משה עניו מאד מכל האדם אשר על פני האדמה" "And Moses the man was more humble than any person on the face of the earth..." (Num. 12:3), the reader generally understands this as praise. Yet a common theme in biblical literature is the phenomenon of a biblical figure's outstanding feature serving as both his claim to leadership and ultimately the key to his downfall. This theme is particularly evident in the major characters of the book of Judges.

Moreover, the inverse nature of the parallel is indicated and underscored by the appearance in each story of two sets of parallel terms differing only in gender. In Moses' journey to Egypt he stands beneath the **ass**, *hamor*, that bears his family; Baalam rides atop the **she-ass**, *aton*, that will topple his presumptuous pride.[27] The instrument through which Moses will learn that his sense of inadequacy and its resulting hesitance are wholly inappropriate will be the **son of Tziporah**—literally: "son of a female [bird]" (בנה).[28] The instrument that fulfills the opposite literary function in the journey of Baalam—namely, the inflation of his ego so that he presumes that he can transcend God's mandate—is identified as the king Balak **son of Tzipor**—literally: "the son of a male bird." In both stories, the bird is the very apt symbolic representation of transcendence or upward flight. For Moses, Tziporah (literally: female bird) and her son convey the message that the gravitational pull of mortal limitations (of being heavy-tongued) can be defied and transcended. For Baalam, the son of Tzipor (bird) seduces him into the mistaken egotistical belief that his prophetic abilities and powers of speech can transcend God's will. The switched genders of the *hamor* and the *aton*, as well as that of *ben Tzipor* and *ben Tzipora*, together with their juxtaposition in the plot of the stories, were subtly deployed in these verses both to refer readers to the relevant parallel text and to indicate the inverse nature of the comparison.

The inverse parallel between the two stories could be summarized by the following equation:

---

[27] In fact, at the revealing of the divine threat, Baalam is forced to dismount and bow to the ground (Num. 22:31).

[28] Recall that the circumcised child is referred to as בנה—**her son,** and not as Gershom, Eliezer, "their son," or "his son."

172

	Moses	Balaam
Problem:	Humility	Hubris
Solution:	Tziporah	Aton
	Brith Milah	Prophecy and Speech
	(raising the humble)	(humbling the proud)
	"השפלה הגבה"	"הגבה השפיל"[29]

While the two stories present opposing personalities, with opposite problems, there is a commonality in the way they evoke God's wrath. In the case of Moses, inappropriate humility is tantamount to hubris as he attributes inflated significance to his own abilities (or lack thereof) in the mission of liberation from Egypt. The message of the twin stories is that the messenger can neither do more nor less than what God asks of him. The prophet is ultimately a vehicle for the divine will, and can neither transcend its dictates with his inflated self-importance, nor ground its transcendent message with the weight of his inappropriate humility.[30]

Returning to the additional parallel noted by Rashbam—that of the threatening divine wrestler at the Jabok crossing—we now begin to recognize the existence of a distinct biblical genre of "internal struggle" stories. In each instance, as we have indicated, on the eve of fateful confrontations, biblical heroes meet their internal demons and wrestle with their own evolving identities through the simulation and transference of artificial confrontations with divine messengers. These are stories of journey, of

---

[29] Both of these phrases—"raising the humble" and "humbling the proud"—are borrowed from Ezekiel 21:31. See also Proverbs 29:23, I Samuel 2:7, Job 5:11, and Psalms 147:6. In these verses and elsewhere, the juxtaposition of *raising the humble* and *humbling the proud* represents a frequently emphasized biblical theme.

[30] With regard to Tziporah's pronouncements in Exodus 4:25–26, we direct the reader to the article by Joshua Blau, mentioned in note 18 above. Blau's thesis does not contradict our contentions, but rather provides an additional layer of meaning to the episode at the lodging place that goes beyond the scope and focus of this chapter.

transition, and in both cases the geography and the forward/backward dance represent psychological territory lost and gained. There inheres, at the lodging place (*malon*), as at the Jabok crossing, a story of the complex negotiations between the divine plan and human efforts.

In one case, we witness Rebecca's reliance on the divine promise and Jacob's relinquishing of autonomy both to Rebecca and to his perception of divine fate. The result: a crippling of his autonomous moral sense to the detriment of the very promise of "Abraham's blessing" they had connived to appropriate from the blind Isaac. In the case of Exodus 4, Moses hoped to advance the cause of the divine mission by passing it on to more capable hands—in the end forcing an exasperated compromise that involved the reliance upon a wondrous "staff of God" and upon the superior oratory of Aaron. His faulty negotiation of the interplay between the divine plan and human efforts again brings about detriment to the very cause he intended to further. A common denominator of these tales is the apparent lesson that Jacob and Moses can neither fulfill their own destinies nor advance the covenantal destiny of their people by the route of circumvention. Confrontation with self is a *sine qua non* for confrontation with the other, and ultimately, for blessing and for redemption.

The essence of these stories is not the external confrontation that is the usual stuff of historical drama. These will take place on the morrow —when Baalam faces the plains below his perch and utters blessings, when Jacob meets up with his brother Esau, and when Moses comes before Pharaoh. In the internal struggles—these bouts with self and identity—advances are subtle, partial and tentative. Territory must be won over and over, and name-changes are not final. Moses seemingly backslides when he persists in calling himself "uncircumcised of lips" even after the lesson of the *malon*. Jacob continues to be called Jacob and continues to act in a *Jacobly* fashion, not only subsequent to Jabok, but even after the confirmation of the angel's name-change by God himself in Genesis 35. Similarly, Baalam persists in following Balak (apparently still in the hope that he might overcome God's restrictions on his speech), even after the episode with the speaking *aton*. The Bible demonstrates a keen appreciation for the nearly deterministic weight of human psychological constrictions. Yet the arena for heroic transformation remains the subtle, and at times imperceptible, territory within which one becomes "enabled" (ותוכל).

Moses will indeed continue to see himself with an extreme humility that is at once his most important qualification for prophecy and at the same time an Achilles heel in terms of his political leadership.[31] We have posited the literary relationship between "heavy of tongue" and "uncircumcised of lips" as synonymous phrases that decode the mystery and non sequiturs of Exodus 4. However, the nuance that separates these metaphors is also worthy of consideration.

What has Moses learned if the didactic trauma—of the divine threat and Tzipora's dramatic circumcision of their son—leaves him with the same sense of inadequacy that had plagued him beforehand? Bluntly, if the symbolic act of circumcision was intended as an antidote to his inappropriate self appraisal as "uncircumcised of lips," it clearly hasn't worked. Moses continues to refer to himself as uncircumcised even after the incident at the *malon!* The answer may lie in the evolution of self awareness that is reflected in the change of language Moses uses to describe his limitations.

---

[31] The conflicting prerequisites for prophecy and for political leadership—of lack of ego and of substantial ego, respectively—are both inherent in the paradoxical situation of Moses as prophet and king. As prophet he is susceptible to the breakdown of personality that results whenever a mortal being is exposed to infinite light. In fact, all prophets seem to be devastated at the first experience of prophecy and need to be rehabilitated by God before they can serve as His messengers. Disintegration of self is related to the reduction of ego as the infinite divine presence makes one aware of the infinitesimal stature of his or her fragile ontology. As Moses' level of prophecy is potentially the most dangerously devastating to mortal ego, God must choose as the object of his most intense revelation a nearly egoless human. An ego that is already reduced will not be destroyed by the process of radical reduction. Hence, "the man Moses was very humble, more than any man on the face of the earth" (Num. 12:3). Cf. Eliezer Berkovits, *God, Man, and History* (NY: Jonathan David Pub., 1979) 32–34.

"Heavy of tongue/mouth" and "uncircumcised of lips" are not entirely synonymous. "Heaviness" belongs to the lexicon of the given, of facticity; "uncircumcised" is the language of potential, of the "yet to evolve." The latter is language that suggests and points to the possibility of completion.

In Moses' ability to abandon the terminology of "heavy of mouth" in favor of the more nuanced "uncircumcised of lips" we find evidence of the subtle effect of the incident at the *malon*.

As is the case in Jacob's wrestling at Jabok, evolution of identity and the concomitant advance of covenantal destiny is indicated in the very ability to reframe one's predicament. Victory is not guaranteed nor does the divine blessing or promise obviate the struggle for human autonomy. The territory that has been gained tentatively (and must be continually reconquered) is the space between facticity and potential redemption, between fate and destiny, between the perspectives of circumvention and that of confrontation.

AFTERWORD: EDEN AND AUTONOMY

We have suggested that in the Genesis narratives and in the parallel stories of Moses and Baalam, the objective of the divine plan involves and necessitates the evolving identity of an autonomous human will. This idea is implicit, as well, in the very first biblical narrative—that of the Garden of Eden and the tree of the knowledge of good and evil.

In recent conversation with Moshe Greenberg, he noted the paradox inherent in the story of Eden. The story is, on the one hand, a description of the fall of man and of rebellion against God's command. It accounts for the present, tragic state of affairs that includes travail, sadness, suffering, and subsistence only by the sweat of our collective brow. Eating of the tree resulted in exile from the garden. On the other hand, it is the story of an inevitable advance on the part of humans to a state of being—past innocence—an advance that moves toward an empowering knowledge of good and evil. This knowledge is described (by the narrative itself) as nothing less than divine. "And the Lord God said: 'Now that the man has become like one of us, knowing good and evil. . . .'"[1]

Greenberg noted that even in the eschatological visions of the prophets, a return to the idyllic conditions of Eden (prior to the sin) does not include a return to innocence with regard to the knowledge of good and evil. If anything, moral self-awareness will intensify. In my own working out of

---

[1] Gen. 3:22.

the story's symbolism, the cherubs that guard the entrance back into the garden, blocking access to the tree of life, are still there, symbolizing the irretrievable nature of the advance from innocence.

Rebellion against the divine command can, it seems, paradoxically achieve advance toward the human autonomy necessary for the ultimate purpose of creation—namely, the rededication of an independent moral will to the service of God. Thus, the eating of the fruit of the tree simultaneously produces progress and retrogression, transcendence and downfall.

There is coherence and resonance to this paradox as it reflects a more basic and more essential paradox. The God of Genesis desires and commands submission to His will, but at the same time requires the submission of a will independent of His own. Unless mankind fully possesses an autonomous moral will and freedom of action (that, by definition, includes the freedom to rebel), the dedication or submission of that will to God is meaningless.

Perhaps this is the essential meaning of God creating man and woman in His image—the image of a self-reflective autonomous will, as distinct from the animal world and the rest of natural creation. Adam and Eve, prior to the sin, are as the beasts of the field, unreflective beings, as is indicated by their unawareness of their nakedness (Gen. 2:25). The result of the eating of the tree of knowledge is most immediately signified by their new awareness of their nakedness (Gen. 3:7).

Hence, the serpent speaks truth when it promises the woman that eating the fruit of rebellion will make her "like the God—a knower of good and evil." At the same time, this advance precipitates the distancing of man and woman from God—that means exile, suffering, and anxiety as well as independence and autonomy. For to be like God, means, at least initially, to be independent of, and separate from, God. Indeed, this description strikingly parallels the development of a child away from the parent —with autonomy the goal, and at the same time, transfer of common values, the hope. There too, the advancement has its price in the anxiety of separation, the uncertainty of distance, and the danger of rebellion.

The ultimate paradox of the creation of humans in the divine image and of the story of the garden is that of an *advance that requires a retreat* and *a fall that enables a transcending* of the previous human condition. (This theme resonates later in the biblical record as the phenomenon we have examined of *the injury that enables.*)

Conversely, in several biblical narratives, we witness an *advance that constitutes a retreat* by means of an attempt to subordinate, circumvent or repress one's autonomous moral will for the sake of submission to a divine plan. The attempt to "transcend" the autonomous moral sense results in a fall. It is a **premature** submission both in the sense of it coming too soon and too readily, and in the sense of the submission having skipped over the stage of mature, autonomously moral rumination. Patriarchs and matriarchs may try to advance the divine plan (as in the case of Rebecca and Jacob deceiving their blind husband and father in order to achieve the fulfillment of the prophetic promise "the older shall serve the younger"). However, in subordinating their own moral autonomy to their perception of that plan, they end up inhibiting that very plan, ironically sending the covenantal destiny into retrogression.

This irony, that has provided one of the themes of our Genesis readings, is nothing other than the flip side of the paradox of the "tree of knowledge" story. Whereas in the Eden narrative the human rebellion against the divine will (by means of the exercise of autonomy) constitutes progress, in the later stories human submission to the divine plan (by means of the repression of moral autonomous judgment) constitutes retrogression. In both cases, the paradoxical result is related to the essential dialectic whereby God demands submission to his will, but only if the submission is that of a fully autonomous moral entity.

This same dialectic that stipulates separation and individuation from the source of life as a *sine qua non* for a meaningful rejoining of wills and a higher level of wholeness, is also reflected in the other drama of the creation story. In the symbolism of Adam bifurcating in order to allow for the emergence of Eve, we find again the dialectic of separation that creates distance and anxiety, but also enables the ultimately more meaningful existential process of reunification. As we have seen, even the language of Adam's aloneness (*Adam levado*),[2] and the subsequent taking away of his *tzela*[3] (a *rib* or a *side* of himself) is paralleled in Jacob's encounter at Jabok where he is initially *levado*[4] and winds up *tzolea*[5] (limping or favoring one side).

In light of the fact that in many prophetic passages the relationship of God and his covenantal partners is described as that of husband and wife, we are not surprised that the paradox of the separation (the rebellion of eating from the tree) as *tragedy* on the one hand and as *enabling progress* on the other, is echoed in the story of the creation of woman from man. We also find it neither surprising nor incoherent to find the converse of this dialectic evident in the underlying themes of later Genesis narratives. That is to say, just as in the initial stories of Genesis human beings advance paradoxically by means of rebellion, in the subsequent stories they will also regress by means of inappropriate submission and sacrifice of autonomy and identity.

This is so because the question of autonomous identity is not a *yes* or *no* proposition. The internal struggle for autonomous choice—informed by nature, nurture, and divine providence (but not determined by them)—is a subtle and ongoing affair. No dividing line such as eating from the tree, or exile from Eden, nor release from threatening angels or from Egyptian bondage, can demarcate a permanent zone of autonomy. Autonomous identity is the object of an exquisite and challenging dialectic, not that of total or permanent victory, and the biblical record of this struggle is

---

[2] Gen. 2:18.
[3] Gen. 2:22.
[4] Gen. 32:25.
[5] Gen. 32:32.

faithful to the tentative and incremental nature of the struggle.

If, indeed, we see the mythic symbolism of the first three chapters of Genesis as analogous to the birth of a child and its advance from innocence by means of rebellion, we realize immediately that the formation of the individual and its dialectical (covenantal?) relationship with the parent does not end there.

The birth of an infant does not close the chapter of the formation of the individual, but only signifies its separation from the mother physically. Likewise, adolescent rebellion as a necessary advance toward individuation is only an additional step toward discovering and exploring the slippery relationship between past and present, between submission to fate and creation of destiny. In this dance of "away from and back towards," in this constant renegotiation of the covenantal relationship, there will be tragic "errors" of navigation both in terms of rebellions that advance and of unreflective submissions that cause retreat.

The entire book of Genesis might be seen as a divine anthropology or mythic birth and maturation of humanity. The range of successes and foibles that map out the parameters of this ever present dialectic of separation and reunification prepare us for our own participation in the great drama of wrestling with the human and the divine.

About the Author

Rabbi Shmuel (Steven) Klitsner, a student of the late Nehama Leibowitz and co-author of the acclaimed novel *The Lost Children of Tarshish*, has trained a generation of Bible students and teachers at Jerusalem's Midreshet Lindenbaum College. His film credits include the award-winning Hannukah animation, "Lights."

The Essential Writings of Abraham Isaac Kook

Ben Zion Bokser, editor and translator

The Essential Writings of
Abraham Isaac Kook

Edited, Translated and Introduced by
Ben Zion Bokser

Back in print after 18 years!

"This work excels both in its judicious selection of texts... and the quality of the translation. The reader is treated to Rav Kook's views on such topics as culture, evolution, scientific change, Torah study, holiness, morality and the Zionist revival. This volume enables readers to feel the pulse and power of this remarkable thinker."
—David Shatz, Professor of Philosophy, Yeshiva University

Back in print after 18 years, this second volume of Rabbi Bokser's translations of Rav Kook (the first is part of The Paulist Press Classics of Western Spirituality series) consists of letters, aphorisms and excerpts from essays and other writings. Together, they provide a wide-ranging perspective on the thought and writing of Rav Kook.

With most selections running two or three pages, readers gain a gentle introduction to one of the great Jewish thinkers of the Twentieth Century.

Ben Zion Bokser, the translator of this volume, heard Rav Kook speak at Yeshiva University in 1924. Rav Kook became his inspiration, and Rabbi Bokser introduced the American audience to his teachings.
978-0-9769862-3-2 / Trade Paperback, 6x9, 220 pp. / $19.95

The Yeshivat Chovevei Torah Tanakh Companion to the Book of Samuel:
Bible study in the spirit of modern and open Orthodoxy

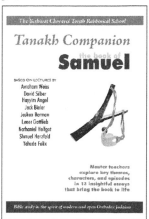

Rabbi Nathaniel Helfgot, editor
based on lectures by **Abraham Weiss,
David Silber, Hayyim Angel,
Jack Bieler, Joshua Berman,
Leeor Gottlieb, Nathaniel Helfgot,
Shmuel Herzfeld** and **Yehuda Felix**

"Almost every chapter of this collection taught me something new about a book that I thought I already understood very well. Creative thinking and wide learning characterize the essays."
—Rabbi Jack Riemer, co-editor, *So That Your Values Live On*

Thirteen eye-opening close readings of the Book of Samuel offer refreshing new perspectives on familiar stories while always remaining true to the text. These essays combine modern literary techniques–the search for parallels and other patterns–with insights from midrash and subsequent classical Jewish Biblical scholarship. Edited from lectures presented at the Yeshivat Chovevei Torah Rabbinical School "*yemei iyun*," this highly readable volume provides a "big picture" understanding of the Book of Samuel through close attention to even the smallest details.

Targeted Hebrew texts are included with translation, so that readers at any level may study comfortably even if caught without a Hebrew bible for reference.

Rabbi Nathaniel Helfgot, editor, chairs the departments of Bible and Jewish Thought at the Yeshivat Chovevei Torah Rabbincal School in New York.
978-0-9769862-4-9 / Trade Paperback, 6 x 9, 268 pp. / $19.95

CPSIA information can be obtained
at www.ICGtesting.com
Printed in the USA
FSOW03n0813081116
27122FS